THE TOWN

That Haunted Hemingway

The Slip and Fall of Young Ernie's Spirituality : The Gradual Corruption of America's Literary Genius

By:

David Wyant

Printed in the United States of America
Wizard of Walloon Press

ISBN 9780990464914

www.wizardofwalloon.com

Table of Contents

Poetry by David H. Wyant

Winter.....71

Spring.....86

To:
Pastor Bernthal, my favorite pastor

August 15, 2014

Best wishes

David Wyant

Petoskey

MI

Introduction

When I say haunting, I mean that in a good way. Unforgettable impressions of Petoskey always persisted in the mind of Hemingway. That's the kind of haunting to which I am referring. As a result, this sleepy, Northern Michigan hamlet often served as the setting, and many of it's characters appear in the author's finest works.

The most complex person to ever live in Petoskey has probably been Ernest Hemingway. To ask around town, one will get dozens of conflicting impressions of him. Old timers will state that the guy was quite the boozing rounder. Others might react negatively to stuff he wrote about their relatives, especially those from Horton Bay; however, the very persons he made into steamy characters always understood and never were upset. They were mature enough to give the guy poetic license with what he wrote.

Then, there are folks who only read *Old Man and the Sea* because it was required reading in High School Literature class. Any original thinking beyond *Cliff's Notes* they gathered from *The Tabloids,* which glamorized his macho life style just to sell copy. Tabloids still have not changed in that regard, but it is my hope that after reading this you can form your own intelligent decisions and be spurred on to want to read his other works, now that you know with what he had to deal.

I want to see a revival of his genius.
I want Petoskey to awaken to honor Hemingway in a proper

fashion.

I want readers to reach again for one of his many prize
winning novels and really begin to understand his
timeless messages.

It is my desire that the reading of *The Town That
Haunted Hemingway* will do just that.

This volume will also reveal that Hemingway's fist love was
not writing novels, but was writing poetry.

Since my love of writing usually takes the form of poetry, I
wanted the reader to share some of Ernest's first
attempts, which also were poems.

With the addition of my own poems, I hope to vindicate
Hemingway from drifting away from his early poetry
vision as a lad, which was pure as the driven snow.

Most people never had a clue that Hem was actually more
of a poetry affectionato. He actually sold him poems before the
novels caught on. His favorite poet was Kipling. One evening
he surprised his friend by reciting from a book by Browning.
Eventually his friend went to bed but he continued all night
reciting the works of the great poet Browning out-loud. The next
morning, Ern was still there reciting, and still orating Browning
with unusual energy, enthusiasm, and dramatic inflection.
Ernie's dream was actually to be decorated as a great Poet
Laureate. Having stated that, one would agree that all of his
work did indeed have a certain poetic rhythm to it.

I think we also should agree that Hem must have been very
psychic due to his deep insight into the world of his characters.
I became psychic after I "died" too, just as he must have at his
wounding in WW1. The concussion of trench mortar exploding
near him, sent his spirit right out of his body and thus made him
psychic thereafter. Psychic as he was, he therefore must have
tapped into principalities over-hanging Petoskey. The Bible
refers to this concept:

In Ephesians 1:19, Paul talks about God's great power. It
was the power that God used to raise Jesus from death. With
that power, he defeated his enemies. Paul uses the same
words here— power, strength and might. We are at war against
our enemy, the Devil (Satan). We therefore need all these

qualities. But we need something more. You must wear all the armor that the Lord gives to protect you. Then you can stand against the evil attacks of the Devil.

When Paul was in prison, they chained him to a Roman soldier. Therefore, he could always see the soldier's armor. But our weapons for war are not weapons with sharp points like a sword. They are weapons of the Spirit. You need these so that you can stand against the evil attacks of the Devil. The word used here is 'stand'. It is as if you are in a castle. It is the castle of the church of Jesus Christ. You are guarding the castle against all the clever and evil plans of the enemy. This war is different from a war with weapons like guns. This battle is not against people. It is against all kinds of 'spiritual forces'. They are in a world that you cannot see. We are not fighting a human army, but we are fighting against the powers of this dark world. We are fighting against the rulers, authorities and PRINCIPALITIES...evil spiritual forces in the heavens. These evil forces will use people to do their evil work. The war is against the Devil and his armies. These armies consist of many different kinds of spirits.

Ernest must have been guided by God to come to Petoskey to fight these Principalities; these spiritual forces in the heavens above the frontier town.

It is my view that Hemingway's whole life became a poem. I used my psychic ability to tap into his style of poetry by adding to what I'd like to think might be considered his continued poetry repertoire, i.e. forest animals, birds, war, death and political topics of the day.

Sensitive as he was, I also point out that he attempted to keep his sanity through his writing. Writing helped him ventilate and re-write negative incidents to his own liking. Psychologists today are just discovering the effectiveness of this cathartic form of Therapy. Ernie was doing it a hundred years before it was discovered by present-day shrinks.

Freud was active in Paris when Hemingway was there and the entire field of Psychoanalysis relied heavily on free association and dream analysis. The majority of *Torrents*, in my understanding, is just that. It was Hemingway's release of repressed material that he was too reticent to publish in any other form. Because the writing of *Torrents* only took him ten days, this is further proof that this novella needed little research, it was stashed in the deeper layers of Hem's psyche.

In October 1885, Freud went to Paris on a fellowship to study with Jean-Martin Charcot, a renowned neurologist and researcher of hypnosis. He was later to remember the experience of this stay as catalytic in turning him toward the practice of medical psychopathology and away from a less financially promising career in neurology research. Charcot specialized in the study of hysteria and susceptibility to hypnosis, which he frequently demonstrated with patients on stage in front of an audience. Freud later turned away from hypnosis as a potential cure for mental illness, instead favoring free association and dream analysis.

After experimenting with hypnosis on his neurotic patients, Freud abandoned it as ineffective. He instead adopted a form of treatment where the patient talked through his or her problems. This came to be known as the "talking cure", and its goal was to locate and release powerful emotional energy that had initially been rejected or imprisoned in the unconscious mind. Freud called this psychic action "repression", and he believed that it was an impediment to the normal functioning of the psyche, even capable of causing physical retardation which he described as "psychosomatic". The term "talking cure" was initially coined by a patient, Anna O., who was treated by Freud's colleague Josef Breuer. The "talking cure" is widely seen as the basis of psychoanalysis.[1]

All this talk could well explain the same phenomenon taking place on a city wide scale in **Petoskey** at this time. A Psychologist's couch not being available, the whole town free associated upon each others ears. This activity still persists in many corners of the town. A good place to witness this is at Julienne Tomatoes. Over an excellent coffee, two can sit in soft easy chairs and have a free, mutual peer counseling session right in the restaurant. It is quite a wonderful thing to behold, and encouraged by Julie[2], whom I counseled with about this regional phenomenon.

Julie Adams of Julienne Tomatoes, a restaurant in downtown Petoskey dedicated to Petoskey Storytelling. An original Petoskey building which was once Schilling's Feed Store and then the Cornwell Beef Company during Hemingway's days in Petoskey.

GFS Marketplace is another good place for a free "talk session." The sales force is taught to "probe" the customer in order to better service their shopping needs. Needless to say, these sessions often get more involved into personal life issues. Friends will gather around the free coffee area to have an impromptu session for long periods.

However, Hem's most pleasurable personal stress escape valve, of course, was fishing and hunting: both terrific stress relievers. We know he never missed a trout season right up to the end.

I suggest the reading of this short volume as a Hemingway Primer. Let it serve to unravel some of the Hemingway mystery and mystique that has lurked between the lines for so many years.

Few analysts take a close look at Hem's second novella. As a bonus to you dear reader, I include an in depth look at what F. Scott Fitzgerald considered a masterpiece, even though it took a swipe at his style along with numerous other authors of that ilk.

"The Torrents of Spring was a satirical treatment of pretentious writers. Hemingway submitted the manuscript early in December 1925, and it was rejected by the end of the month. In January, Max Perkins at Scribner's agreed to publish The Torrents... in addition to Hemingway's future work. Torrents... was published by Scribner's in May, 1926. The first edition had a print-run of 1250 copies. Hemingway received a mixed reaction to the novella that was sharply critical of other writers. His first wife, Hadley, believed the characterization of Anderson was "nasty"; Dos Passos considered it funny but didn't want to see it published; while Fitzgerald considers the novella a masterpiece. The Torrents of Spring has seen little scholarly criticism as it is considered of less importance than Hemingway's subsequent work."[3] My attention to the unusual piece will sneak up on you due to its having escaped analysis for almost a hundred years.

My analysis of *Torrents* is sound and solidly backed up by existing evidence never understood before. After reading my multilevel approach, utilizing period music, as well as a recent avant garde painting, I think the reader will agree that *Torrents* is much more than a "funny book" or a biting parody of Anderson in order to be rejected by his publisher Livermore.

I found Hem accidentally using *Torrents* as a stream of consciousness, which allows us to peek into his own prejudices, his own personal couch session, his own surreal nightmare, which when taken as such, reveals to the reader his literary genius. Psychology was in its infancy at this time and also had its conception in Europe. Freud, who lectured in Paris during Hem's day, even may have seen him in his audiences. Siggy, could have had a field day with the lad.

Fortunately for us, Ernest was way ahead of Freud's findings and packaged his subconscious onto, page for page, some of the world's finest literature; A practice he never quit. I think one must agree that the genius of Hemingway even expanded on Freud's study of mass-hypnosis by making his books so compelling that millions of readers could not put them down.

Dear reader, I especially wanted you to gain a deeper insight into Hemingway's summer home of **Petoskey** and the way principalities, which hover above cities, influence us all.

Where you spent your youth, or where you live now, will have deep impact upon you all of your life due to the influence of over-hanging Principalities.

It is my intention that these factors and a proper understanding of Petoskey might serve as an eye opener toward a more enjoyable snuggle with Ernest's prize winning body of literary work.

Dedicated to my Mother and Father, Leonora and Julius Wyant.

Acknowledgments

*T*hanks given to God for inspiring this work.

Christel Bassett, trusty loyal typist, photographer, and editor in chief.

Ernest Hemingway Mainland, nephew of Ernest Hemingway, for helpful hints during lunch.

John Hemingway, grandson of Ernest Hemingway, for the encouraging emails.

All the written Hemingway biographies and sibling biographies for their inspiring information.

Petoskey public library, where I researched many times.

James Vol Hartwell of Walloon Lake, for his volumes of information on Prudence Boulton.

Members of the Green Sky Hill Methodist Church for allowing us to visit Prudence's gravesite.

John F. Kennedy Library for the public domain photos of Ernest Hemingway.

To all the talkative storytellers of Petoskey, for their kind cooperation and unusual propensity toward storytelling, which inspired and impacted heavily upon a young man named Ernie Hemingway, thus transforming American Literature as we know it.

I

The Town That Haunted Hemingway

Herein lies the key to a deeper understanding of what Ernest Hemingway was trying to do with his writing. Most influential upon his style was the spirit that lives in a beautiful Northern Michigan hamlet. This sleepy little community, born out of the late 1800's logging industry, gave shape to a whole new wave of literature in America. This was the Mecca for a radical new form of writing, but most historians and American Literature experts have no clue that this quaint little town exists, yet it did in fact spawn not one but two Pulitzer recipients and one Nobel Laureate. Bruce Catton and Ernest Hemingway.

While Ernest (winner of both the Pulitzer and the Nobel in 1954) was just a summer guest, Pulitzer winner, Bruce Catton, born the same year as Hemingway (1899) was a native to this town. How many little towns can boast two Pulitzer winners and a Nobel winner for literature? Not too many, I am sure. Let us investigate why this is true.

A proper understanding of this peculiar town, it's citizens, and how it became the setting for a ground breaking, prize-winning style of American novels will enrich the reader seeking to unlock a truth heretofore untold. By understanding what goes on in this town the serious reader and analyst of American literature will hold the key that will unlock a whole new world.

Downtown Petoskey Michigan

Few people realize that every summer Ernest Hemingway spent the first twenty two years of his young life right here in Northern Michigan in, and around our beautiful town on Lake Michigan called **Petoskey**. The whole town was and still is full of "story-tellers." This propensity for unusual social discourse has perpetuated now for at least a century. It reached a cleverly organized peak during the Bay View heyday in 1920, says a whole hamlet full of celluloid- collared, stuffed shirted yarn spinners.

During this time the G.R.&I railroad pulled thousands up here from all over Illinois, Indiana and Missouri to view an outdoor live Indian play called "Hiawatha." Dozens of hotels catered to all the many guests and during this era P-Town was just a 'buzzin.' The Hemingways were among the saucer-eyed visitors. They befriended the Indian actors due to Doctor Clarence Hemingway's affection for Indian culture and artifacts. He had a sizable collection of arrow heads and potsherds. Ernie built a rather unstable birch-bark canoe and playfully sported an Indian jump suit, complete with fringed sleeves and pants.

Anyone residing in P-Town during this period had to be affected by this grand addiction for historical anecdotal narrative. **Petoskey** even boasted its own Chautauqua movement(a noteworthy speaker was William Jennings Bryan.)

By the late 1800's, the Bay View Association had become a pioneering institution in public education. It boasted an ambitious summer university, a Chautauqua series attracting tens of thousands of visitors, and a home study program enrolling men and women across the nation. During this period, the raw territory where the early "tent city" was built was transformed into a resort community of such Victorian charm that in 1987, Bay View was designated a National Historic Landmark.

No less than four hundred and forty four Victorian mansions (most dwellings on other circuits were tents) and gingerbread bedecked "summer homes" were erected and clustered around the main lecture auditorium, thus giving testimony to the draw that a good **Petoskey** ear-waxing had for these folks.

A fascinated young Ernest (already fancying himself a yarn spinner) had inquired of the Bay View director to be a speaker within the circuit, but was rejected and told to learn more and get more writing training. To this day the lecture trend continues in Bay View, but on a lesser scale. That director who refused Hemingway must have felt rather foolish to later hear of Ernest's international fame.

However, this **Petoskey urge to spiel** has now spilled into the streets and has found alive and well in most of it's quaint little shops and homes.

Just as an experiment walk into any shop in town and there will be someone who will fill your brief moments with the grandest screed (a term Hem used in slang) you ever heard.

Stop in for a haircut and before you realize it, your barber or stylist, as they are now called, will probably weave the most beautiful vignette in rhythm with his scissors, the beauty of which, will match your new hairdo. Drop in for a martini at Perry Hotel's Noggin Room or City Park Grill and before you can start sucking the pimento out of your olive, the bartender will intoxicate you with a 100 -proof joke or his triple-sec life story as a chaser. Light up a Phillies Cherute cigar at the Smoke Shop and before you can blow your first smoke -ring, the clerk will start in on a well-wrapped rap that will take your mind off the rasping in your throat. The town was named after a local, high cheek-boned, Ojibwe fur trader from Harbor Springs, named, Chief **Ignatious Ped-a-se-ka,** who has his own interesting story. Full of righteous indignation he abandoned his association with Harbor Springs Jesuits in favor of an early settlement across the bay, to a place called Bear Creek.

The chief planted fruit trees, cultivated large fields, grew many food crops, fished, hunted, trapped and carried on fur trade with neighboring Indians and other settlers. Somehow, he and his wife had 10 children, so in effect he started his own village. He and his sons owned a number of shops (one of which is now Grandpa Shorters).

Grandpa Shorters

In Chief's honor, folks now began calling the place, Pedaseka, instead of Bear Creek. Eventually the name got shortened to **Petoskey,** so white men could pronounce it. A huge principality of thought still hovers over this community as a result of the chief's impressive fight for freedom, sensibility and social solidarity. [*see Ephesians 6:12...Ephesians 6:12*] *For our struggle is not against flesh and blood, but against the rulers, against the authorities, against the powers of this dark world and against the spiritual forces of evil AKA principalities* *in the heavenly realms. Eph. 3:10 To the intent that now unto the principalities and powers in heavenly places might be known by the church the manifold wisdom of God.*

This fact might explain why townsfolk still feel obliged to talk your ears off; they're picking up thought patterns from the ethers above **Petoskey** where Chief and his former priest still slug it out; however, now that everyone has their face stuck to a cell phone or are distracted by any number of other hand-held electronic devices, that trend of friendly conversation with folks we pass on the streets seems to be doomed to extinction. It's only a matter of time before nobody will even know I'm here. Dogs, cats, and other pets are already feeling abandoned. Let us make a conscious decision while in **Petoskey** to shut off our cell phones and portable electronics in honor of the social discourse that used to thrive here.

"Progress" in today's electronics aside, the astute Hemingway student will notice that Chief's themes are exactly the same ideals Hemingway eventually chose to write about. Ernest admired such courage, manliness, struggles overcoming great odds, war and the drama of death. He was a social/romantic activist and originator of his own universe, a pragmatic moralist, and knew how to last and convert a carefully cultivated stoical fortitude into the stuff of which heroes were made.

Chief and Hem would've been great buddies. It seems quite natural how a sensitive kid like Ernie would have absorbed all of these issues, since they just floated around above town like a domed cover over the area. Ernest simply had to sit and listen to what was being transmitted from the ethers around **Petoskey**. Each town has its own set of principalities. **Petoskey's** seems to have been set there by the strong convictions of the chief pursuant to his emphatic break with the over zealous Jesuits of Harbor Springs.

Now around this same time Chicago's demand for building materials had reached it's way up to Michigan. They were lusting for our giant, untouched, virgin forests. My Dad (who was about the same age as Ernie) recalls that some pines were so huge that four men could barely reach around their trunks.

It was not long, and Pedaseka's quiet fur trading town gave way to the denuding sound of ax and woeful whine of hungry saw mill. The focus of shore line fishermen was interrupted by the sight of large billowing sails of giant Great Lake schooners seeking dock-age in order to tote away the large piles of virgin, fresh cut pine and oak-destination... Chi-Town.

Petoskey's protected bayside location, together with it's natural lake harbor, made a few pot-bellied lumber barons in town prosperous when logging was begun at the turn of the nineteenth century. They flaunted their wealth by sucking their teeth and disgustingly picking roast beef out with their unending supply of tooth picks.

The region's abundant, giant, virgin pine and oak trees were laboriously logged, hauled to lumber mills and then the large beams, planks and boards were transported out by schooner or rail.

Railroads and later steam boats not only hauled tons of giant, prime Michigan lumber to build Chicago's homes, but during summer also brought back with them many over-heated Chicago tourists to escape the heat. One such sweaty visitor was, Dr. Clarence Hemingway, his wife, daughter and infant son, Ernest, from a wealthy Chicago suburb called, Oak Park, Illinois. Here they found relief from the stifling, Chicago, summer heat; while also being captivated by northern Michigan's breath- taking beauty, its abundant fish, game, fresh fruits and vegetables.

The cool Lake Michigan breezes and this dynamic, local, story-telling quirk also spawned the Bay View Association, built about the same time period. It still operates as a summer Methodist, Victorian village formed during the Chautauqua (story-teller) lecture movement. Current topics of interest are still presented in the lecture auditorium throughout the summer.

The Bay View Association of the United Methodist Church was founded in 1875 by a group of Methodists to be a retreat. An educational program of lectures and music began in 1886 and the community developed around these activities.

Bay View is known for its Victorian style cottages and peaceful scenery. This small community consists of 30 community owned buildings, 440 cottages, 2 hotels and a post office. Also a beach (with a swim area), a children's pool at the beach, a sail house, a recreation house, and Boys and Girls Club program.

Two historic inns in Bay View are the Stafford's Bay View Inn and The Terrace Inn Bed and Breakfast. The Terrace Inn was built in 1911. The Stafford's Inn was built in 1886.

The Terrace Inn

The camp was listed as a National Historic Landmark district in 1987 as one of the best-preserved examples of the Methodist Camp Meeting movement, as originally built in 876, and then adapted to the Chautauqua movement in 1885 through 1915.

II

The Pride of Petoskey

Bruce Catton and Ernest Hemingway

B ruce Catton, another local Pulitzer winning Civil War story-
teller also originated from Petoskey. Catton praised "the
stand-up valor of the private soldier." His readers began to
appreciate that he was doing something different from earlier
Civil War historians: The heroes of his books weren't so much
the generals and men of rank who issued orders, but the grunts
who did most of the actual fighting. Catton relied heavily on
their thoughts and observations, drawn from regimental
histories and other sources. He approached his research like a
good journalist: He interviewed old soldiers, took careful notes,
made sound judgments, and relished in the discovery of
colorful quotes and detail, much the same as Hemingway
gathered his topics and character studies.

"During the thirties, we rented cottages on Crystal Lake for
two weeks or more almost every year," says Bruce's
son,William. The visits would have been longer, but Catton
always needed to get back to a desk in a faraway city. Then, in
1954, he "hit the jackpot," as his son puts it. *A Stillness at
Appomattox,* the final volume in the Army of the Potomac
trilogy, won the Pulitzer Prize and the National Book Award.
Civil War buffs continue to recognize it as one of the finest

books ever written on their favorite subject.

David McCullough, the author of *Truman, 1776, John Adams,* and other bestsellers, has described his own experience of reading *Stillness at the Appomattox* as a senior at Yale: "I think it changed my life. I didn't know that then, naturally. All I knew was that I had found in that book a kind of splendor I had not experienced before, and it started me on a new path."[4]

"Bruce Catton (1899-1978) was a Civil War specialist whose early career included reporting for various newspapers. In 1854 he received both the Pulitzer Prize for historical work and the National Book Award. He served as director of information for the United States Department of Commerce and wrote many books, including Mr. Lincoln's Army (1951), Glory Road (1952), A Stillness at Appomattox (1953), The Hallowed Ground (1956), America Goes to War (1958), The Coming Fury (1961), Terrible Swift Sword (1963), Never Call Retreat (1966), Waiting for the Morning Train: An American Boyhood (1972), and Gettysburg: The Final Fury (1974). For five years, Catton edited American Heritage."[5]

A Bruce Catton plaque with his portrait in bronze stares quizzically in front of Carnegie Library in downtown, Petoskey, his hometown. No Ernest Hemingway plaques exist as yet, but a donor has been found and we will soon see a life sized bronze statue in a park. One large Motor Vehicle Department sign was recently erected in Lake Walloon park.

Carnegie Library, Petoskey MI

Unfortunately, only one small corner of **Petoskey's** original, old railroad depot displays the Hemingway family pictures and books. As of yet, there is no northern Michigan museum dedicated to the Nobel Laureate's illustrious writing career. Eventually, I predict a Hemingway festival, statue and a permanent school for writing will emerge when people discover the power of this region to create story-tellers.

III

Hemingway, The Youthful Story-teller

Only ten minutes away from, Petoskey, along **Lake Walloon** hides the family cabin which was inherited by Ernest's nephew. It is surrounded by huge multimillion dollar homes that resemble corporate conference centers. The little 20 by 40 foot family retreat now looks terribly out of place.

To protect the nephew's privacy, no one will tell you where Hemingway cabin can be found, so don't even ask!

On rare, well planned, occasions the retired insurance salesman has been known to guide a small group of well mannered reporters or television crews through the historic cottage.

Horton Bay (fifteen minutes away on Lake Charlevoix) proudly, but quietly, boasts Ernie's 1921 marriage to Hadley Richardson, where remnants of the occasion can still be found in pictures, booklets and memorabilia at The Red Fox Inn. One can even purchase a shirt with Hem's image in full beard and quote; saying, "Just write one true sentence!" Pitifully little else can be found in Michigan which honors America's most famous author.

Papa Schlept Here

Hortons Bay General Store

The most dynamic novelist of the 20th century, who won the Pulitzer and Nobel prizes for his gripping literature, has precious little dedicated to him and his achievements for being a resident during two decades of his formative writing career. Yet even though he traveled to excitingly romantic Paris, Italy, Spain, Switzerland, Bavaria, and throughout Europe as a successful newspaper correspondent, still, most of his novels all carried images, characters, impressions, and expressions he soaked up, as a sponge of a boy, growing up in the **Petoskey** region. **The town really haunted him! The haunting, though, was in a good way.**

Hemingway's idyllic summers in Petoskey obviously were unforgettable. Those cherished and precious moments got so deeply infused in his young mind and his vibrant blood that he could not shed them in order to write about some other topic.

Young Ernie Fishing

Even while lavishing in romantic Paris, surrounded by the world's greatest *avant garde* Art and architecture, towering cathedrals, famous painters, poets and noteworthy expatriate novelists of the century, he still wrote compellingly about the woodsy, adventurous **Petoskey** character (biographical we all think) whom he called, Nick Adams. Young Nick, was always pictured against a backdrop of the tall picturesque pines and bubbling pristine springs and rivers of Northern Michigan.

Living in Paris, Ernest, was daily drinking and dining with *avant garde* literary powerhouses like; F. Scott Fitzgerald, James Joyce, Ezra Pound, and Gertrude Stein while also receiving bold encouragement and incessant influence from groundbreaking artists like Chalder, Miro, and Picasso, but it did not affect him as much as that early mental, Michigan imprinting. He always had Michigan on his mind, using it as setting and its citizens as story characters.

In a letter to his best friend Bill Smith, Hem admits this haunting as follows (text in brackets are my explanations);

"I know how good all our old stuff-[story-telling] was Bird [Bill]because everything, almost everything worth anything I've written has been about that country [Petoskey, Michigan]. It was the whole darn business inside me (the haunting) and when I think about any country and doing anything it's always that old stuff, the Bay[Horton's Bay], the farm, rain stein fishing, the swell times we used to have with Auntie [Mrs. Charles] at the farm, the first swell trips out to the Black [river] and the Sturgeon[river] and the wonderful times we had with the men [Michigan story-telling folk] and the storms in the fall and potato digging and the whole thing, and ...[here's the haunting]...we've got them all[the story-telling style] and we're not going to lose them..."[6]

Wherever Ernest wrote, the Michigan storied imprints pervaded. It was a truly beautiful haunting; however, few would put together the true psycho/sociological facts unless one were sensitive and had spent some time living here in this peculiar town to absorb the colorful idiom and anecdotal aberration.

The famous writer also admits to this haunting in many other letters to friends like: Carl Edgar, Jacques Penecost, Fever Jenkins, Brummy Brumback, that any and all of his best work has been about life in northern Michigan, that same old business of the bay (Horton's), the farm, fishing, hunting, swell trips to the Black River, the Sturgeon River, the storms, the potato harvest, pitching hay at Walloon Lake, the barn dances. He confesses that the country life adventures of Michigan got in him and even though he has seen some stunningly beautiful country, like Italy, France, Spain and the picturesque mountains of Austria, he cannot get clear of his charming Michigan story-telling memories even if he tried. Trying to do so would be like telling a fuzzy duckling not to line up to follow his Mother. The imprinting is just too deeply rooted.

On his honeymoon with Hadley atop the crest of **Petoskey's** Eppler Road, overlooking the wide expanse of Little Traverse Bay, Ernest stopped Earl Bacon's car, asked Hadley to step out while romantically stated to her that he had seen the beauty of Naples, but no place was more beautiful than, **Petoskey's Little Traverse Bay** in its autumn colors (and where he gave a most captivating story; that was his ticket to Toronto).

His bride was well aware of his captivative story-telling. After all, had he not just talked her into marrying him?

Little did she know that she too had to get up-dated in her story-telling technique, or Ernie would soon find another woman who would. Little did she know how strong an attraction story-telling was for her young husband. History would show that he eventually went through three more wives all for the same search— for a captivating woman who told equally captivating stories. *Torrents of Spring,* Hem's personal psycho/nightmare drama, reveals this pattern in the character called Scripps, as he loses interest in Diana, while being attracted to Mandy, due to her truly captivating story-telling.

Ernest grew up the oldest boy, surrounded by four sisters, an infant brother and domineered by a frustrated diva of a mother who relegated domestic chores to servants and cooking to her husband. After a few years family discord drove Ernest to seek solace outside the Walloon Lake cabin. As soon as he was able, he slept in a pup tent during the evenings to get away from it all. It was in that tent that he read volumes of all his favorite storybooks. In that tent he could be near his friends like, Tom Sawyer, Huck Finn and the Native Americans. Evidence all points to the fact that Ernest had a love affair with Prudence Boulton, a fifteen year old Ojibwe girl. Myth has it that Prudence died giving birth to Ernest's child. I found her grave near Horton Bay.

Prudence's Grave near Green Sky Hill Church

His first love was Prudence Boulton. Being a half-breed she was considered an undesirable because of the social stigmas placed on whites fraternizing with any Native Americans.

Ernie more than likely had a relationship with her, but society being what it was then, nothing more could happen. Here then, was another source for a haunting. Her memory had to interfere and cast a big shadow upon all his relations thereafter. Her all-pervading memory may have led to the ruination of Hem's many marriages. He would have constantly been comparing his loves with the ideal of Prudence and her native beauty and tribal charm which he idealized in his mind (Mary Hemingway recalls in her memoir Hem's remark about her legs being almost as nice as Prudie's). Consequently, true to his style of Journal Therapy he (as Yogi in "Torrents") takes off his clothes and heads down the tracks with the naked squaw, thus fulfilling his fantasy to be reunited with his first love and join the liberal Pagan scene he so longed for all of his life.

Ernest's Naturalist tendencies peaked each time he experienced the excitement of hooking a big, scrappy Horton Creek trout, a Walloon Lake walleye, winging a plump grouse or pheasant, or dropping a rabbit, deer, or bear to provide wild game for his family. He then broke any silence in the quiet little town by telling everyone he met about his heroics. It was so Ernie because it was so **Petoskey. At the mention of fishing or hunting around here, you have at least an hour of exciting stories waiting for you!**

Ernie's favorite expression as a child was,'"Fraid of nothin'"and he proved that axiom many times throughout his eventful life.

His Michigan fishing and hunting adventures set the stage for what was to eventually lead to larger international adventures, but the youthful mastery of his Michigan adventures molded him and gave him the necessary skills, personal confidence and raw-boned courage that was needed to later hunt and stare eye-to-eye with danger and much larger game while on safari in the vast plains and teaming jungles of Africa. Of course, telling about it became an obsession also. Often, he confessed that he always felt compelled to write something every day.

Teenage Ernie Fishing

He ate whatever he bagged in those steaming jungles (like filet of lion) yet his thirst for story telling was never quenched quite as nicely as a cold glass of delicious, Horton Bay, Michigan apple cider.

And so it was that the relating of these unique experiences, the high adventures impressed upon the sensitive boy during his formative, "growing-up years" in our **Petoskey** region gave rise to early poetry(which I want to revive), and compelling short stories that later spawned a talented, hard-boiled novel writing style. It was that heavily haunting influence of **Petoskey's way of thinking**, that typically Michigan can-do attitude, sense of humor, hospitable charm, warm culture and concise idiom that shaped the century's horseless carriage industry, radio, telephone, telegraph, and air travel.

As we now know, it also became the spawning grounds for the century's most classic novels which emerged from the blossoming mind of our boy, Ernest. It was those seed-bed adventures, those friendly, nurturing (more so than his own family at times, especially the Charles family of Horton Bay which he referred to as Auntie and Uncle, Hem's life-long best friend Bill Smith was their nephew whom they helped raise) northern Michigander people relaying those special regional sights, cultural frontier attitudes, Native American ways, tribal affections, smells, tastes and sounds that became branded deeply into Hemingway's sensitive and furtive alchemical mind. Those precious geographical boyhood, memories— which are uniquely Northern Michigan— produced a century's most gripping stories (many turned into Academy award winning movies), from the pen of our summer native son of twenty years, the young, handsome, creative, Pulitzer and Nobel Laureate, our Ernest Hemingway.

Herein lies many of the **uniquely Petoskey**, unforgettable, regional, story-telling tastes, sights, sounds, flora and fauna which got so stuck in the memory of our most famous visitor; thus explaining, why it still remains…

The Town That Haunted Hemingway.

IV

It Started with Poetry

Hemingway's first writing attempts started with simple, yet powerful poems:

Poetry was Ernest's first love and it is easy to understand why he wrote over 80 different poems. True to the memory so powerfully etched in his hiking of the area, the following group of poems follows the footsteps of the famous writer. Just image what it must have been like for him.

Travel Hemingway's poetry trail with me. Stroll through those same forests and finish his legacy of poems like Hem may have done. Wander along the same river trails, gaze across the same misty vistas, the same spectacular distant horizons watching the birds, wildlife, and weather patterns, and spring into the joyous wonder of verse. Sometimes we will just sit on a big stump, listening to our inner voices, imaging what Ernest must have seen when the giant tree was virgin, standing proud and tall a hundred years ago when he roamed these woods. We can listen to the clear-throat, lilting bird calls (which he loved so much), take in the fresh smells of spruce, of blossoms and new-mown hay, hear the splash of fish jumping in the streams. It is still possible to understand that all his future fame had its inception in the picturesque Petoskey area for it's unspoiled natural beauty still inspires thousands. Let it inspire you today through our **Petoskey- region poetry**.

Here is one of Ernie's first poems, written in rhyming couplet fashion while he was only twelve and in grade school. He has had twelve summers of listening to Petoskey yarn spinning and now he proudly tries his hand at it. His mother cherished it and saved it for us to enjoy now:

The Opening Game
(12 April, 1912)
"With Chase on first, and Evers on third,
Great things from the Cubs will soon be heard.
Then up comes Schulte to the bat,
On the plate his bat does rap;
Takes a slug at that old ball,
Makes it clear the right field wall.
Then in comes Chance and in comes Evers,
Such hits are seldom seen—'most never.
Then to the bat comes Zim in haste,
He sure knows how the ball to paste.
He slams that ball upon the bean,
Almost seems to make it scream.
The center fielder nabs the ball;
It seems as if 't'would make him fall.
But stop of this rank stuff,
Just one inning is enough."[7]

Five years later, at age seventeen, Ernie, wrote for his high school literary journal, *Tabula.* This next rare poem is one of my favorites. It is timeless and is fashioned after James Whitcomb Riley's work:

The Inexpressible:
(EH 1917 *Tabula* March)
"When the June bugs were a-circlin'
Round the arc light on the corner
And a makin' shooty shadows on the street;
When you strolled along barefooted
Through a warm dark night of June
Where the dew from off the cool grass bathed your feet-

When you heard a banjo thunkin'

On the porch across the road,
And you smelled the scent of lilacs in the park
There was something struggling in you
That you couldn't put in words-
You was really livin' poetry in the dark."[8]

There it is!
Did you see the haunting?
He assimilates all what uniquely stimulates the senses of our region and then converts it into a fine poem about **Pennsylvania Park in downtown Petoskey**. What most of us would hardly take note of, or at best give a, "Oh, isn't that cute?" young Hemingway writes a penetrating discourse suitable for printing in *Down Beat*, *Jazz Digest*, or any other popular Art, Music or Poetry magazine of the day.

It is amazing that at the tender age of seventeen, Ernie had already become an Alchemist. A few years later he would revolutionize 20th Century literature.

In his own young way he had figured out how to convert the love of God expressed in and through nature and put it into words. Young Hemingway must have witnessed and heard celestial symphonies and was determined to become a living poetry—a conduit— for God's rich and abundant love for his people in their intoxicating tribal, woodsy setting. He saw his Mother's Bible lessons come to life in a veritable **Petoskey Garden of Eden**. How profound! Ironically this theme would stay with him until the end, for after his untimely death, *"Garden of Eden"* did finally become published posthumously. but now we can see where he got the motif. He was always trying to work in those idyllic days in the **Petoskey woods.**

Our hundreds of summer visitors search for this feeling, some find it, but some are so busy shooting across the bay on jet-skis or frantically shopping for souvenirs, Christmas presents, and fudge that they miss it entirely.

On numerous occasions during summer vacations from Oak Park High, Ernie and a few pals would travel to **Petoskey** on foot, sleeping in pup tents and feeding off faith and their nimrod- fishing skills, testing dozens of abundant trout streams along the way.

His sisters, Marceline and Ursula, recall also steam-boating ahead of the family in order to meet Ernie and friends in **Petoskey**. Obviously all three had the same haunting which was to be in **Petoskey** where they could be away from the overly protective parents and just let loose telling and hearing newly captivating stories. They enjoyed their close, adventuresome teenaged friends and played tennis, baseball, fishing, boating, hiking and picnicking in Petoskey and Charlevoix, as well as Hortons Bay.

Marceline, the oldest child, who was also touched by this **Petoskey-story-telling** phenomenon did in fact originate a successful nation-wide lecture tour during which she told captivating stories about opera and the popular Broadway theater stars. She later married and built a cabin near the family cabin, Windemere, on Walloon.

After graduation from High School, Ernie, landed a reporter position for the Kansas City Star due to his uncle Tyler's connections there. Although his tenure at the Star was short (six months) he became a successful newspaper stylist chasing the news all over Kansas and gaining valuable experience which would propel him into Paris later on.

The Kansas City Star Building where Hemingway (and later Harry Truman) worked was located at the northeast corner of 11th Street and Grand Avenue.

"Truman worked in the mailroom wrapping newspapers here for two weeks in August 1902. He made $7.00 the first week and $5.40 the second.
He left to take a job as timekeeper for a construction company working for the Santa Fe Railroad. In later years, Truman sometimes differed with the Star. "If the Star is at all mentioned in history," he wrote in a letter to the Star which he never mailed, "it will be because the President of the U.S. worked there for a few weeks in 1902." (Letter to Ray Roberts, June 12, 1950.)[9]

Later when WW1 broke out, Ernest, driven by patriotism and a need for adventure, left Kansas and joined the Red Cross as an ambulance driver on the Italian front. During the very first rounds of artillery exchange at the Fossalta di Piave front, Hem, (considering himself invincible), was severely wounded by trench mortar and machine gun fire.[10] Somehow he managed to rescue an Italian soldier and hauled him over a hundred fifty yards to safety, even though Ernie's legs had stopped over two hundred pieces of lead.

He recouped in Milan after numerous operations to remove all the shrapnel and machine gun bullets. Our young hero was awarded Italy's highest medals and during his stay at the hospital, fell madly in love with his nurse, Agnes von Kurowsky.[11] They pledged to be married.

Hem returned home alone on January 21, 1919 in order to heal, but they kept in contact by prodigious letter writing.

In March of that year our wounded hero traveled to **Petoskey** due to the opening of fishing season. He stayed off and on through that summer at Windemere, and Horton Bay.

Hem suffered a deep inner blow when Agnes sent him a "Dear John letter", breaking off their affair by wanting to marry an Italian Lieutenant. Ernie, was emotionally shattered and psychically crushed; however, while in Horton Bay he managed to meet, Marge Bump, probably on the rebound and probably at Dilworth's famous chicken dinners in Hortons Bay, where she waited tables.

As we all know, rebound romances never last and this one was no exception, but Ernie had to cling to someone at this juncture. He picked apples and potatoes in the area for quick cash that fall. He was also receiving insurance money from the Italian government.

Guy C. Conkle, M.D. who had an office in nearby Boyne City remembers treating a hobbled, cane-laden, Ernie for shell shock and two hundred twenty-seven shrapnel wounds the summer of 1919. Doc remembers that he stayed at Dilworth's in Hortons Bay for a while, but later took a room in Petoskey and checked into Eva Potter's rooming house at 602 State Street in Petoskey. Dr. Conkle recalls that as a patient, Hem was brave , brilliant, but nervous, constantly telling stories about fishing, hunting, and many interesting things. Doc suspected he may have taken a fragment through the scrotum which also got him wondering about his manhood.

602 State Street, Petoskey, MI

We assume the move to, **Petoskey**, was mainly to be near, Marjorie Bump, who at seventeen was still attending Petoskey High School. She had red hair, dimples and was very active in literary activities. The school was conveniently only one block away.

Her relationship with Ernie never got past the platonic stage, even though he was quite smitten by her. My guess is she told a good story. Years later she married a dentist.

It is suspected Ernie did eventually sow his wild oats during this time with a waitress on the docks near Hortons Bay for he describes quite graphically a similar scene in *The End of Something* which was so explicit that he had trouble getting it published in America.

A poem which could well have been written in **Petoskey** during this healing period reflects his sexual ambivalence after the war:

Killed...Piave
(July 8 1918)

Desire and
All the sweet pulsing aches
And gentle hurtings
That were you,
Are gone into the sullen dark.
Now in the night you come unsmiling
To lie with me
A dull, cold, rigid bayonet
On my hot-swollen, throbbing soul.[12]

Ernest not only needed to heal a wounded leg, but also needed to mend a broken heart and he needed desperately to prove his manhood and prove to himself that he had what it takes to be a good story teller through writing— his career of choice.

Hazel Potter, Eva's daughter, remembers that he was typing away all the time up stairs, in his front corner room...he saw only one girl; namely, Margie Bump. While waiting for school to dismiss he would hang out at McCarthy's[13] barber shop by the flat iron building downtown near the tracks. Story telling is always at its best in the **Petoskey** barber shops.

Georgianna Main Dickinson '47 chronicles the friendship of her mother Lucy Marjorie Bump and Ernest Hemingway through letters, photographs and interviews in her novel Pip-Pip to Hemingway in: Something from Marge.

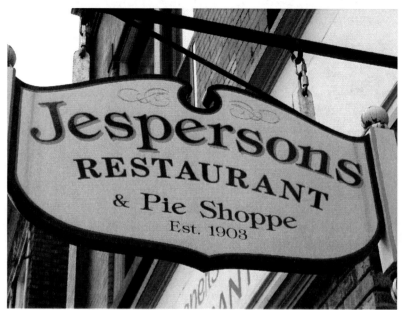

Jesperson's Restaurant and Pie Shoppe, Est. 1903.
Famous for their Banana Crème Pie!

He took his meals at nearby, Braun's Beanery[14] (Best By Test, first floor of New Braun Hotel, 210 Howard Street) which became the setting for *Torrents of Spring*[15]. Patrons and waitresses (recalling his Margie Bump) became icons of story-relating skill for him and he included them in *Torrents...*

His main character of that early novella, Scripps O'Neil, marries the older waitress Diana(a symbol of Hadley and the old story- telling style of the day), who re-tells literary magazine gossip, but eventually he is more attracted to the better story teller, Mandy (with Pauline in mind), whom he now loves mainly because she speaks from her own experiences. It rings true to Scripp's ears and he is captivated (see *Torrents...*p. 93)

There it is and even more clear this time.

Unmistakably... he was there for the story- telling.

Closing lines of,*Torrents...* repeated lines of story-telling by Mandy the buxom waitress succeed in mesmerizing Scripps and also author Hemingway in real life around **Petoskey**.

Jesperson's Restaurant was across the street and is still

baking the best pies in town. No doubt he digested plenty of story telling over there as well. The owners tell of his stops for coffee.

Pictured Author David Wyant, with Jesperson's owners, Bobbie Jesperson, and husband Mayor William Frazer

A lady in charge of the girls dorm at Bay View let him type in one of the vacant rooms. She stated that she couldn't resist his good looks and disarming manners, even though it was against all policy and social rules of the day. Again, another example of his ability to tell a good story and change policy even in the ultra conservative Methodist women's dorm of the ultra conservative Bay View Association. His skill of being able to craft a story and make it believable was building momentum.

He may have taken a few meals at Terrace Inn while on Bay View campus. They now have dedicated a Hemingway room in his honor. Hem's actual fishing rod is fashioned into the curtain rod, his actual creel and landing net can still be found there also. One of Chef's outstanding dishes features a Hemingway chicken breast smothered in cherry sauce as a permanent item on their menu. I have tasted it and it is now my favorite. Mo Rave, the owner, will gladly show you around the well preserved, old inn.

Hem, and his teenage sisters often arrived in **Petoskey** before their parents. Often they all were guests at the Perry Hotel which still stands due to its fire proof brick construction. Many huge Petoskey hotels of wooden construction burned down decades ago.

The Perry Hotel, Petoskey, MI.

I had drinks at the very bar stool Hem sat on at the Annex, now called, The City Park Grill. He was known to spend many hours writing on his notepad, sipping gin gimlets (with a twist of lemon) while sharing stories and pumping the bartenders to reveal there respective life-changing experiences so he could use them in future books.

Hemingway's portrait on the wall at City Park Grill

While enjoying a pleasant lunch with, Hem's nephew, Ernie Mainland, he commented that Hem often shot pool and engaged in bare fist fights in the backroom where there still can be found tunnels used to stash booze during prohibition. His pugilistics not only made him popular with both men and women, but also served to convince and change people's minds in his direction. He often considered boxing as a profession.

Ernie commented, "I put in a fall and half a winter writing up in Petoskey. I worked and wrote and couldn't sell anything."

Aha! Maybe nothing sold then, but the powerful ideas hatched during this monumental winter of discontent in **Petoskey** later were bought months later by *The Toronto Weekly Star* and gave birth to numerous prize winning short stories like the Nick Adams stories, especially *Three Day Blow, The End of Something, Up In Michigan, Torrents of Spring*[16] and led to his first great novels, *A Farewell To Arms and The Sun Also Rises.*

Torrents... **setting takes place entirely in the town of Petoskey.**

Of monumental importance here at this time in Hemingway's healing is Agnes von Kurowsky's fateful rejection letter. She accidentally had done the world a great service! That powerful little document served as another "trench mortar" explosion in Ernie's soul. It's deep emotional shock and its tragic suffering spurred our Ernie on to great heights in order for him to overcome the great sadness and severe depression she had caused.

It was at this time, because of Agnes' rejection, during his physical and emotional convalescence in **Petoskey** that **Hemingway charted a serious course to become the world's greatest writer**. During his **Petoskey** recovery a teenager named, Marj Bump, also spurned his suit, but she always remained a lifetime family friend, especially of Ursula Hemingway.

In *The End of Something* we see Nick break up with a Marge at the suggestion and encouragement of his friend "Bill" (modeled after, Bill Smith, his life-long literary friend). No doubt this was Ernie's way of re-doing the rejection that Marjie Bump inflicted upon him.

For Whom the Bell Tolls was to be his way of re-writing the damage of Agnes. This powerful story became a popular movie starring Gary Cooper and Ingrid Bergman.

Noteworthy, here we see Ernie using Journal Therapy as a form of recovery a whole century before it was invented by psychologists. I find that remarkable! In fact this therapeutic avenue continues in *Torrents...* although meant as a parody/funny book, can now be looked at as Ernest's confession of a desire for tribal sexual freedoms, his dream for the future of his real character development, and his purely authentic writing style. Charles Scribner's publishing of *Torrents...* not only announces a clean break from Hem's old chop -happy publisher (Boni & Liveright) but puts all of his critics and teachers on notice that Mr. Ernest Miller Hemingway can now cut the muster as a man and as the Jaw Bone of his generation. Nothing can take the wind out of his sails from here on out. He will be dancing in his "Tails"(through his Tales) struttin' in his top-hat from now on!

Hemingway's distinctive writing style is characterized by economy and understatement, and had a significant influence on the development of twentieth-century fiction writing. His protagonists are typically stoical men who exhibit an ideal described as "grace under pressure." Many of his works are now considered classics of American literature.

During this pivotal healing period of his Petoskey convalescence, hero Hem, gave a life-changing talk at the downtown Carnegie Library. Still using a cane, dressed in full Italian uniform, with shiny brass buttons and stunning black cape, wearing his polished knee-high Cordovan leather boots, Ernie captivated his naive audience of Ladies Auxiliary. Carefully he crafted and outlined his tragic WW1 wounding.

Seated in the quietly enchanted audience was an impressed, Mrs. Ralph Connable, a family friend. On the strength of that speech she hired the war hero to travel to Toronto as a tutor for her crippled young son, Ralph Jr. They all stayed in the Connable mansion. Hem tutored for five months in Toronto. During that time, Mr. Ralph Connable (a Canada Woolworth department store executive) introduced Ernie to the editor of the *Toronto Star Weekly.*

Ernie hung around the press room and impressed editors with his Kansas Star experiences; enough to sell them a number of good stories he had typed in **Petoskey**. When his time was up with the Connables he returned to Chicago and shared an apartment with some literary pals from Hortons Bay.

It was at this time, unknown to literary historians, that he wrote probably his best poem. It is only one stanza long, yet in it's condensed brevity it conveys the entire theme of the post WW1 Lost Generation which had its inception at this time in history:

Chapter Heading
(Chicago, 1921 from *"Three Stories and Ten Poems"*)

For we have thought the longer thoughts
And gone the shorter way.
And we have danced to devil's tunes,
Shivering home to pray;
To serve one master in the night
Another in the day.[17]

It was about this time that Ernest met Hadley Richardson, and married her later in 1921 at Hortons Bay. Soon after, *The Toronto Star* hired him full-time and shipped him and his new bride off to Paris on assignment to capture the post-war European recovery efforts.

Sherwood Anderson, whom Ern met in Chicago, wrote him a priceless letter of introduction which opened doors for adventures and influential Art and literary friendships there in Paris. Here he would discover that he had what it takes to be the world famous literary figure which we now know, but his topics, characters, and hard-boiled style were always mined and refined from the **Petoskey** region of Michigan.

When family life pressures got too much for Ernie, Michigan's wild forests gave refuge to our stressed out young author. It was while hunting in our forests that Ernest felt closest to God. He saw God's majesty reflected in Michigan's virgin forests much as one would be in awe walking into a huge cathedral. It struck him with Providential amazement and respect to stand beneath the high canopy of Michigan's majestic pines and worship their God- given, towering greatness while shafts of sunlight filter through their massive, outstretched branches. God's wilderness was a sight much more impressive to him than the man-made, multicolored light that filters through the stained glass windows of Notre Dame or Chartre cathedrals in France. His goal was to capture nature in writing the way Cezanne painted landscapes— bold, abbreviated, with clarity and just a hint of a much bigger truth.

Even when he was in Paris, Ernie's thoughts were bringing him back to barefoot memories on his family farmland of Walloon lake and the many exciting adventures along its railroad tracks. In his next poem we see revealed the very religious side of Ernie. At twenty-six he sees God, the fool for love, revealing Himself through nature as a never ending, all flowing gland.

Here is another of his couplet- rhyming parodies on Joyce Kilmer's famous poem,"Trees".

I *Think That I Have Never Trod*...
(N. Y. Times Mag, Paris 1926)

"I think that I have never trod
On anything as swell as sod
Sod whose hungry heart extracts
The wisdom of the railway tracks
Sod that underneath thy feets
Produces pumpkins trees and beets
That lies on mother nature's breast
And gives the meadow lark a nest
Trees are made by fools like God
Who pushes them up through the sod.
For God is love and love is sod
Let all unite to worship God.
And let the Maker's trembling hand
Emulate the ductless gland
Thus are we in His wisdom brought
To see the things that God has wrought.[18]*"*

Far more inspiring than his urban home of Oak Park, Illinois was Ernie's Michigan summer life adventures. Never did he write about Oak Park (he referred to it's wide yards and narrow minds), but this poem reflects images all found around his summer home, **Petoskey,** in Northern Michigan and he praises God for them.

His Up North fishing and hunting of wild game was his way of worship and praising God continually. Ernest's wild-woods, Michigan exploits not only took him away from the critical eye of his female-dominant, overly religious family, but also served as mental therapy. Recently scientists have discovered the need of children to play outside. No- child- left- inside is a recent movement expanding on that research, but Ernie practiced it all too well up in **Petoskey**.

I found this was his uniquely personal form of spiritual redemption. When the affection was not forthcoming from Mother and Father, he turned to his Heavenly Father for the consolation he needed and would slip out of his shoes and socks (he hated to wear socks) to walk barefoot, to kneel on God's earth to make a bed of cedar bows and rest in between fishing and hunting adventures. For, Ernest, a wild-woods breakfast of fresh caught trout, fried in bacon, followed by homemade riverside, buckwheat pancakes and apple butter was the best communion meal there was. For our Ernie, this was church. To him a successful fish or hunt was redemption and the act of writing was his cathartic form of therapy as well as his confession. (see *The Sun Also Rises*)

V

"You can get the boy out of, Petoskey, but you can never get Petoskey out of the boy!"

My experience of walking the very ground and railroad tracks where Ernest walked as a shoeless youth has given me access into Hemingway's fertile and creative mind. It feels like channeling the same muses which he had discovered.

Writing in a religious vein like he did also made me feel much closer to God every time I took my notebook into his **Walloon** woods, along his favorite clear rivers or along his personal, pristine lake shore.

So in order to get the most benefit from the pages that follow, try to lift your spirits through the inspiration offered by the unique Michigan scenes. Let my descriptions of the rich soil, the abundant flora, the mysterious fish, fauna, birds and picturesque people be fresh, as if seeing them for the very first time. Imagine being impacted deeply as if you are that same young, wide-eyed, sensitive, complex youth. He survived and became an over-comer, in spite of being dressed as a girl during infancy, masqueraded as his older sister's twin while attending school in Chicago, raised by a frustrated artistic, operatic diva who imposed music lessons and strict Bible lessons on him at an early age.

He adored his doctor father, became inspired by Dr. Clarence, studied ornithology, botany, etymology, biology, fishing, hunting and taxidermy, yet was somewhat disappointed by Dad's lack of courage in the face of his domineering wife, Grace Hall Hemingway.

Daily play with his neighboring Indian friends gave Ernie stalking skills which he utilized all his life thereafter during the hunt, during war, in revolutionary tribal uprisings in Spain, Italy, Africa and hunting German U-boats in and around Florida.

As viewed and understood from this, **Petoskey context**, it will become quite apparent why I chose the title for this work and it will also enrich your understanding of Ernest's later themes as found throughout many of his award winning novels.

Images uniquely northern Michigan, specifically, **Petoskey's story-telling legacy**, will begin to stand out. Social tribal discourse, short, choppy, Indian dialog, regional dialect, regional hunting and fishing techniques, Michiganian sense of humor and point of view will become apparent; thus, advancing your future understanding of hidden messages beneath Hemingway's storied themes.

The more one understands of **Hemingway's timeless Petoskey,** the richer will be the reading enjoyment of all his work. This volume will then become the missing primer that has been vitally needed for a deeper, richer, spiritual aspect of the much analyzed author. **The more we know about, Petoskey,** the more we will know about Ernie and his entire body of work.

It has been said, **"You can get the boy out of Petoskey, but you can never get Petoskey out of the boy!"** Eventually the reader may even feel the need to visit this unusual region some day for your own edification just so you can better learn to read between the lines of his poetry and prose. Meanwhile, please allow my imagery in regional verse to capture the same feelings that affected our most decorated young author.

Ernest and I -both exposed to the same haunting that is Michigan's- also share a similar life path, parallel in many ways and contexts. We both had near death experiences, his during WW1 from a shell burst, (he recounts how his soul left his body like a silk handkerchief being lifted by the corner out of a jacket pocket) mine as an eight year old drowning in the Ocqueoc River-(I went up the tube of light, heard the fabulous Celestial Music, saw Jesus and heard him say,"What have you done with your life?") I shrugged my shoulders as if to say,"Not much."

Sometimes I feel this death experience similar to Ernie's, gives me an advantage over other writers who have tried to do biographies of him. It is quite easy for me to touch into Hemingway's spirit because of our mutual adventures into spirit world.

I attended college in Hem's backyard of, River Forest, Illinois, married in Oak Park, drove Chicago trollies and buses throughout Chi-town and can truthfully attest to unique regional influences in both locales; Oak Park and **Petoskey**.

So it is, that daily now, while living in **Petoskey** I find myself drawn to walking the trails where young Hem traversed. I touch into the vibe, the inquisitive nature of the complex, impressionable kid, caught in a new century of changing values, changing life styles and changing morals. He had before him a new millennium desperate for change in content and also in writing styles. I have found out why Ernie became: "The Jawbone of a Generation."

Oily Weather
by Ernest Hemingway

The sea desires deep hulls—
It swells and rolls.
The screw churns a throb—
Driving, throbbing, progressing.
The sea rolls with love,
Surging, caressing,
Undulating its great loving belly.
The sea is big and old—
Throbbing ships scorn it.[19]

VI

"The Jawbone of a Generation!"

It was while in **Petoskey** that Hem decided to become that harbinger for which the new century clambered. Petoskey served as his spring-board. It helped him put into words their yearning voices. Living in the town of story tellers, **Petoskey** made him become the jawbone, their personal story-teller, of that searching, "Lost Generation" fresh out of the devastation that was left by WW1

Ernie's writer friend and Paris mentor, Gertrude Stein, later labeled him and his friends, "The Lost Generation"because his writing style rejected hers[20] and snubbed his nose at all of the popular writers of that time as exhibited in his second novella *Torrents Of Spring*[21].

I find my passion now is trying to find out what made him that way? What happened to the young, Ernest Hemingway? What impacted him during his youth that perhaps laid the foundation for such a talent? If I could, I would bottle it, but I have a suspicion it was regional, the out of doors, the sights, the sounds, the soil, the water, the wild game meals, the long, meditative, primeval wildness of the **Petoskey** area and it's indigenous, story-telling people.

This territory and society shaped him into the prize winner that he became. He saw life from both sides(family and wilderness interaction) and drew from both in his writing style, characters and themes.

My mission is to analyze, crystallize, define the Alchemical composition and describe it in such a unique way as to give the reader a profound dose of the same subtle medicine, the same brew, the same magic potion and codes hidden between the lines which just may trigger another such "jawbone for this new generation", this new century, that is heavily upon us in all its glory, glamor, and notoriety. Our troubled new generation sorely needs a truthful literary mouthpiece and that writer just may be spawned by a timeless examination of **Petoskey** as it was 100 years ago as experienced by an Alchemist called, Ernest.

Hemingway's move to Paris at this tumultuous time in the early nineteen hundreds exposed the sensitive young man to monumentally dynamic changes in all the Arts. Art historians have failed to totally capture what can best be described as a conscious un-doing of what Art had been up to that time. Painting itself saw the birth of the tremendous changes called cubism, abstract surrealism, impressionism, and many others too numerous to mention. Art for art's sake had it's inception at this time.

Music also took radical swings from the past. One such swing was too much for anyone to hear. In fact audiences rioted violently while hearing Igor Stravinsky's *Rite of Spring*. This famously upsetting performance was held just down the street from Hem's Paris address. Good reporter that he was, it must have tweeked his interest tremendously, especially with his more than casual interest in music established by his Mother.

Stravinsky's images are echoed in *Torrents...* i.e. page 7... "times when he was drunk the sound of the whistles of the trains at night pulling up the Boyne Falls grade seemed more lovely than anything this chap **Stravinsky** had ever written." Pagan life style of Scripps and his first wife, the naked squaw serves as the maiden which is sacrificed all of which are to be found in *Rites...*Hem's reference to that riotous piece of, so called, music may still have brought on a chuckle back in 1925.

Not only is music influencing Hem's second novel but modern painting also lets him get free to personally express his inner tribal yearnings and help resolve his nightmares of style as a modern writer. Once again, **his work becomes effective**

Journal Therapy.

Painter Joan Miro, a Paris friend of Hemingway's just had revolutionized the painting world with his invention of abstract surrealistic, psycho/nightmare illustration.

Miro had invented a style all his own. Ernest admired the bravery of his friend for this departure from what others now were painting so his friends helped him purchase Miro's *The Farm*, and it hung quizzically on the wall of the Hemingway bedroom. They admired it not only for his visual enjoyment but because it inspired him to do likewise with literature-—to create an abstract, Pagan, surrealistic psycho/nightmare. He knew the power of this work!

Hemingway's *Torrents of Spring* achieves all that and also cleverly thumbs his nose at all the expatriate artists, exasperating writers, disturbing critics, sorry analysts and unrelenting literary gossip magazines of the day.

Ernest's, *Torrents...* incorporates all of Miro's lack of proper perspective and radical departure from accepted rules of order even includes a little Miroesque bird (see center of painting)into his intoxicating story.

Supercharged by the study of the inventive impulses of Miro's new expression now hanging on the Hemingway wall, together with all the other shockingly trans-formative changes by Stravinsky in Music, Pagan dance, and all other facets of cosmopolitan Parisian life, Ernest, the Alchemist,charges headlong into the fray with his own brand of radical Literary Art. Of course he remembers his first taste of story-telling success, which was in **Petoskey**; hence that town becomes his setting. Even though *Torrents...* takes him only about ten days to finish what was first meant to be a joke, a bad joke, I find, *Torrents of Spring* to be the most pivotal and most transcendent of Ernest Hemingway's literary works. He was hoping that this, his second novel, would be so shocking that it would propel him out of a constrictive contract (held by his old publisher Boni & Liveright) and onto the waiting liberal presses of Charles Scribner & Son. That novel was *Torrents of Spring,* Ernest's "funny book."

It was to be another of his famous parodies, but this time he made fun of, Sherwood Anderson,(publisher, Boni & Liveright's favorite son). Hem had been experiencing artistic frustration because their editors wanted to cut out vital segments of his works. He was sure they would refuse this shocking second novel, and they did, thus breaking contract with Hemingway's old publisher and paving the way for an enduring relationship with Scribner which lasted the rest of his life.

Poetry was my choice of medium due to a deeply rich, multi-level character inherent in the genre's nature. Hemingway would have said the same, for **Romantic poetry was his first love.** Even his novels are very poetic in nature, but he first wrote over 80 poems. We remember Hem for his novels but I have revived a few of his noteworthy poems. Hem is 22 years old living in Paris; yet, here is a poem in free verse with occasional rhyme that he unleashes of a young **Petoskey, Michigan memory:**

Along With Youth
(Paris, 1922 Three Stories & Ten Poems)

"*A porcupine skin,*
Stiff with bad tanning,
It must have ended somewhere.
Stuffed horned owl
Pompous
Yellow eyed;
Chuck-wills-widow on a biased twig
Sooted with dust.
Piles of old magazines,
Drawers of boy's letters
And the line of love
They must have ended somewhere.
Yesterday's Tribune is gone
Along with youth
And the canoe that went to pieces on the beach
The year of the big storm
When the hotel burned down At Seney, Michigan.[22]"

The Hemingway Family

The poems that follow will trace a graphic degradation from Ernest Hemingway's pure beginnings and eventually unravel in parody, sarcasm, and personal jabs at critics. It is my view that he took himself too seriously and began to use his words as weapons against his critics. A classic case of too much fame. Referring again to Archibald McLeash's answer when asked what happened to Hemingway, he replied that fame happened to Hemingway.

Failing to heed his own advice, which included regular visits to the forest to regain his center, failure to go to church, failure to attend confession, holy eucharist, scripture reading, and association with Christian culture and society. He spent too much time in bars and dives, coupled with too much drinking, and had too many concussions due to plane wrecks. Hemingway failed to protect his consciousness, and filled his mind with things he should have avoided to keep his mind pure. The astute reader of the following poems will be able to grasp that gradual shift in his attitude and his awareness and therein find a personal lesson for themselves. The result of reading good literature inspires, and reading about the writers of good literature can find much to gain from a life that is wasted. Hemingway's later years leave nothing but sadness and despair. When Hemingway's death made the headlines, the entire world was saddened, however that spark of creativity, which he received from his forest muses departed long before his demise. His constant tailing by the FBI via J. Edgar Hoover drove the man crazy.

<u>God is away for the summer...</u>
Society column- The Reverend John Timothy Stone,
pastor of the Fourth Presbyterian Church, has gone to
the Colorado Mountains for the summer.
By Ernest Hemingway

God is away for the summer
The city swelters along without him.
Children cry in the hot nights
Keeping men awake who must go to work in the morning.
The burlesque houses are closed by the heat
Plump women don't look good
In hot weather
Even to the men who frequent the Star and Garter.
John Timothy Stone has followed Him up into the mountains.
In the fall he will be back
He will bring the word of God from the mountains
God never leaves the city for long.[23]

Flat Roofs
by Ernest Hemingway, Chicago 1920-1921

It is cool at night on the roofs of the city
The city sweats
Dripping and stark.
Maggots of life
Crawl in the hot loneliness of the city.
Love curdles in the city
Love sours in the hot whispering from the pavements.
Love grows old
Old with the oldness of sidewalks
It is cool at night on the roofs of the city.[24]

Night comes with soft and drowsy plumes...
by Ernest Hemingway, Chicago, 1920-1921

Night comes with soft and drowsy plumes
To darken out the day
To stroke away the flinty glint
Softening out the clay
Before the final hardness comes
Demanding that we say.[25]

Lines to a Young Lady on Her Having Very Nearly Won a Vögel
by Ernest Hemingway, Chicago, 1921

Through the hot, pounding rhythm of the waltz
You swung and whirled with eager, pagan grace
Two sleepy birds
Preen in their wicker cages
And I
Am dancing with a woman of the town.[26]

Bird of Night
by Ernest Hemingway, Chicago, 1921

Cover my eyes with your pinions
Dark bird of night
Spread your black wings like a turkey strutting
Drag your strong wings like a cock grouse drumming
Scratch the smooth flesh of my belly
With scaly claws
Dip with your beak to my lips
But cover my eyes with your pinions.[27]

Mitrailliatrice
by Ernest Hemingway, Chicago, 1921

The mills of the gods grind slowly;
But this mill
Chatters in mechanical staccato.
Ugly short infantry of the mind,
Advancing over difficult terrain,
Make this Corona
Their mitrailleuse.[28]

FOR THE HARLOT HAS A HARDLOT...
by Ernest Hemingway,Paris, 1922

FOR THE HARLOT HAS A HARDLOT
SYPHYLLIS IS HER END
AND THE HARLOTS PORK
DOES A LOT OF DIRTY WORK
AND THE HARLOTS DOG AINT WELL.[29]

Blood is thicker than water...
by Ernest Hemingway, Paris, 1922

"Blood is thicker than water,"
The youn man said
As he knifed his friend
For a drooling old [bag]
And a house full of lies.[30]

All armies are the same...
by Ernest Hemingway, Paris, 1922

All armies are the same
Publicity is fame
Artillery makes the same old noise
Valor is an attribute of boys
Old soldiers have tired eyes
Al soldiers hear the same old lies
Dead bodies always have drawn flies[31]

Shock Troops
by Ernest Hemingway, Paris, 1922

Men went happily to death
But they were not the men
Who marched
For years
Up to the line.
These rode a few times
And were gone
Leaving a heritage of obscene son.[32]

Roosevelt
by Ernest Hemingway, Paris, 1922

Workingmen believed
He busted trusts,
And put his picture in their windows.
"What he'd have done in France!"
They said.
Perhaps he would—
He could have died
Perhaps,
Though generals rarely die except in bed,
As he did finally.
And all the legends that he started in his life
Live on and prosper,
Unhampered now by his existence.[33]

Riparto d'Assalto
by Ernest Hemingway, Paris, 1922

Drummed their boots on the camion floor,
Hob-nailed boots on the camion floor.
Sergeants stiff,
Corporals sore.
Lieutenans thought of a Mestre whore—
Warm and softy and sleepy whore,
Cozy, warm and lovely whore:
[Darn] cold, bitter, rotten ride,
Winding road up the Grappa side
Arditi on benches stiff and cold,
Pride of their country stiff and cold,
Bristly faces, dirty hides—
Infantry marches, Arditi rides.
Grey, cold, bitter, sullen ride—
To splintered pines on the Grappa side
At Asalone, whre the truck-load died.[34]

To Good Guys Dead
by Ernest Hemingway, Paris, 1922

They sucked us in;
King and country,
Christ Almighty
And the res.
Patriotism,
Democracy,
Honor—
Words and phrases,
They either nagged or killed us.[35]

Arsiero, Asiago...
by Ernest Hemingway, Paris, 1922

Arsiero, Asiao,
Half a hundred more,
Little border villages,
Back before the war,
Monte Grappa, Monte Corno,
Twice a dozen such,
In the piping times of peace
Didn't come to much.[36]

Montparnasse
by Ernest Hemingway's, Paris, 1922

There are never any suicides
in the quarter among people one knows.
No successful suicides.
A Chinese boy kills himself and is dead.
(they continue to place his mail in
the letter rack at the Dome)
A Norwegian boy kills himself and is dead.
(no one knows where the other Norwegian boy has gone)
They find a model dead
alone in bed and very dead.
(it made almost unbearable trouble for the concierge)
Sweet oil, white of eggs, mustard and water, soap suds and
stomach pump rescue the people one knows Every afternoon
the people one knows can be found at the cafe.[37]

The Age Demanded
by Ernest Hemingway, Paris, 1922

The age demanded that we sing
and cut away our tongue.
The age demanded that we flow
and hammered in the bung
The age demanded that we dance
and jammed us into iron pants.
And in the end the age was handed
the sort of [junk] that it demanded.[38]

I'm off'n wild wimmen...
by Ernest Hemingway, Paris, 1922

I'm off'n wild wimmen
An Cognac
An Sinnin'
For I'm in loOOOOOOOve.[39]

Schwarzwald
by Ernest Hemingway, Paris or Germany, 1922

As white hairs in a silver fox's skin
The birches lie against the dark pine hill
They're talking German in the compartment
Now we're winding up
Through tunnels
Puffing
Dark valleys, noisy rivered
Rock Filled, barred with white.
Heavy browed houses
Green fields,
Forested with hop poles
A flock of geese along the road
I knew a gypsy once who said
He hoped to die here.[40]

I Like Americans
By A Foreigner (Ernest Hemingway), 1923

I like Americans.
They are so unlike Canadians.
They do not take their policemen seriously.
They come to Montreal to drink.
Not to criticize.
They claim they won the war.
But they know at heart that they didn't.
They have such respect for Englishmen.
They like to live abroad.
They do not brag about how they take baths.
But they take them.
Their teeth are so good.
And they wear B.V.D.'s all the year round.
I wish they didn't brag about it.
They have the second best navy in the world.
But they never mention it.
They would like to have Henry Ford for president.

But they will not elect him.
They saw through Bill Bryan.
They have gotten tired of Billy Sunday.
Their men have such funny hair cuts.
They are hard to suck in on Europe.
They have been there once.
They produced Barney Google, Mutt and Jeff.
And Jiggs.
They do not hang lady murderers.
They put them in vaudeville.
They read the Saturday Evening Post
And believe in Santa Claus.
When they make money
They make a lot of money.
They are fine people.[41]

Neothomist Poem
by Ernest Hemingway, Paris, 1926

The Lord is my shepherd, I shall not
want him for long.
He maketh me to lie down in green pastures
and there are no green pastures
He leadeth me beside still waters
and still waters run deep
the wind blows and the bark of the trees is wet from rain
the leaves fall and the trees are bare in the wind
Leaves float on the still waters
There are wet dead leaves in the basin of the fountain.[42]

Lines to a Girl 5 Days After Her 21ˢᵗ Birthday

by Ernest Hemingway, Cuba, December 1950

Back to the Palace
And home to a stone
She travels the fastest
Who travels alone
Back to the pasture
And home to a bone
She travels the fastest
Who travels alone—
Back to all nothing
And back to alone
She travels the fastest
Who travels alone
But never worry, gentlemen
Because there's Harry's Bar
Afderas on the Lido
In a low slung yellow car
Europeo's publishing
Mondadori doesn't pay
Hate your friend
Love all false things
Some colts are fed on hay
Wake up in the mornings
Venice still is there
Pieons meet and beg and
breed
Where no sun lights the
square.
The things that we have loved
are in the gray lagoon
All the stones we walked on
Walk on them alone
Live alone and like it
Like it for a day

But I will not be alone, angrily
she said.
Only in your heart, he said.
Only in your head.
But I love to be alone, angrily
she said.
Yes, I know, he answered.
Yes I know, he said.
But I will be the best one. I will
lead the pack.
Sure, of course, I know you
will. You have a right to be.
Come back some time and tel
me. Come back so I can see.
You and all your troubles. How
hard you work each day.
Yes I know he answered.
Please do it in your own way.
Do it in the mornings when
your mind is cold
Do it in the evenings when
everything is sold.
Do it in the springtime when
springtime isn't there.
Do it in the winter
We now winter well
Do it on the very hot days
Try doing it in hell.
Trade bed for a pencil
Trade sorrow for a page
No work it out your own way
Have good luck at your age.[43]

VII

Emmet County, Michigan Makes a Monumental Impact on the 20th Century Literary World

Natural beauty has made the lakeside hamlet of Petoskey the inspiration for hundreds of tourists, numerous summer cottage dwellers, restorers, boaters, and outdoor sports enthusiasts. However, regional beauty touches the sensitive ones on a deeper level. Petoskey can touch the heart.

Like Hemingway, Catton, and many others, it's beauty triggers the inner muse and sets off creativity in an attempt to capture in words this inner impact. God's handiwork as exhibited in Northern Michigan is unsurpassed and daily I was deeply touched by it's panoramic vistas, it's variegated hues, and it's subtle textures.

Hemingway was forever haunted by the beauty of this remote region. The indigenous people and the intuitions they provided shaped his adult life and writing style. What follows is a chance for the reader to share in that same scenery that got under Hemingway's skin and influenced so much of the literary world of the twentieth century. Being daily immersed in this climate and culture, I too, try to capture it in verse. A seasonal pattern emerges and poems are grouped to reflect the ever-changing moods of this region.

The missing ingredient: To totally understand 20th Century Literature, one has to hear about Petoskey because of the effect it had on the most influential writer of the 20th century.

Our prize winning native son, Ernest, has been analyzed by more biographers than any one of his era, but they all miss the mark when they fail to understand the culture from which he emerged, namely, 1900s Petoskey, Michigan.

When the literary world started to read Ernest's work, which was pure Petoskey-ese, it craved more due to it's radically different frontier subject matter, and the clarity of his high impact declarative sentence structure, totally devoid of adjectives and adverbs.

Long, flowery, overly sentimental and naively meandering stories had been their steady diet for centuries prior, but when Hemingway's exciting Michigan adventures hit the readers, it was like a young bear's first taste of honey. They wanted more. Not only were his stories unique, but his character studies were fresh and compelling. They all originated from Ernest's colorful summer adventures in the Petoskey area. His colorful descriptions were like the landscape paintings of Cezanne and Miro. Even the weather was included.

Now we are used to this type of literature, but at the time for 1920s readers, it came as a radical mental shock. Ernie's Michigan formula stunned readers into submission and they demanded more. Hemingway's hard-boiled presentations of Michigan's Petoskey region became like eye-candy for readers raised on milk, toast, pablum, and British biscuits. While his contemporaries like F. Scot Fitzgerald, James Joyce, and others cultivated an audience of the wealthy segment of society, Ernest composed great literary symphonies, utilizing only the seemy dregs of society, to indicate how much degradation had crept into our world. His Petoskey-inspired prose in actuality was creative expansion of his outlandish poetry aimed at a back-to-Eden compass point setting for the common man.

My mission, as I see it, is to remind us where it all started. Where contemporary literature found it's roots; its early foundation. For that we must spotlight that time and place in the life of the most influential writer of the age, and what influenced him, namely the forest primeval of northern Michigan.

This period saw many more national parks set aside

through Teddy Roosevelt. John Muir and photographer Ansel Adams were also hard at work encouraging our return to nature. The clamor of the glamor of urban life was driving people crazy, as witnessed in WWI, where a mechanized country attempted world domination.

Now, along comes young Hemingway, who exposes our folly and while in the midst of our self-made bedlam (Running of the Bulls) takes us away for a fishing trip (The Sun Also Rises). A society caught up in rudderless edge-walking eventually will find itself bankrupt with nowhere to turn.

As spokesman for his time, the jawbone of the "Lost Generation" (Gertrude Stein), Ernest saw his grave responsibility and did his part the best way he knew how, and received Nobel and Pulitzer recognition for those gallant efforts.

Precious little remains of his footprint in Petoskey. The maddening crowds of tourists looking for bargains and eye candy will find little set aside to commemorate where it all began; hence, the humble reminder captured here aimed at a rekindling to that effect. The birthplace of American literature has to be Petoskey, Michigan.

Winter

"All my life I've looked at words as though I were seeing them for the first time." ~ Ernest Hemingway

The poems that follow remind us what could have been if Ernie had persisted on his youthful poetic vision which was inspired by his early religious training and the beauty of Petoskey.

Each poem, written by author David Wyant, in the spirit of Hemingway (not a parody), would stand on it's own merits; however, when viewed as a haunting of Hemingway's, they will take on another mysterious spiritual dimension.

Early fame had blinded Hemingway to ever giving thanks to God for his remarkable talent. Unfortunately, he began to believe his own press releases and the hard-boiled image created by publisher and tabloid alike.

Herein, we find a spirit that serves to polish Hem's tarnished image.

Had his vision stayed Petoskey-pure and had he pursued a personal Walk With The Lord, his poetry might have looked like this:

Bay Front Clock
February 27, 2008

Bay front clock stands
smugly tall
Overlooking boat slip
stall,
Vacant now for one
good reason-
Waiting for a warmer
season.

Petoskey's towering time
piece
Starkly asks us all to
see,
"What have you done
with life's short lease
As viewed against
eternity?"

Dobson, too once
mentioned sly,
"Time flies, you say?
Alas, ah no, time stays,
'Tis we who fly."

Along life's classic
continuum stage,
Where birth and youth
mature to age
Comes fond advice from
English sage.

But, now say I,
Eventually 'tis not time,
but gravity
Which gets us all!
Grinds us down,
Treats all the same,
Backs us all into the
ground
To soil from whence we
came.

Behooves us all
To reason why,
Then ready leave some
legacy
Which lifts beyond
depravity,
Transcends this flesh
and deifies.

Ascend us up to
Kingdom's throne.
Messiah came, the deed
is done.
'Twas in His blood
Where power lay
To lift us all, e'en flesh
and bone,
Transport us to our
rightful home.

<u>Bayfront Birches</u>
February 7, 2007

Imagine my surprise
When right before my eyes,
Shielded from the winter's
breeze,
I found a healthy birch tree.
There it stood!
It made me stare
At its elegant white wood,
And shaggy Afro hair.

At Bayfront Park
We all can view
How its unique bark
Once made a canoe.
With branches strong,
Straight and narrow,
They also make...
The perfect arrow.
Of course the pine

Is very fine.
Stays green
All through the winter,
But I have found
Their arrows bound
And eventually will splinter.
Birch beauty makes the
nicest fixture.
Makes brides pose
To get a picture.

Their grooms stand by
For a shirt tail tuck
In hopes the tree
Will bring them luck.

Birchwood poles

Are fine for fishin'
Makes good cabinets
For the kitchen.

Birchwood is light,
Not real hard-

I'd like to see

A birchtree
In every yard.

If woodpeckers
Would just stay away
There'd be more around
To this very day.

A poet may try
to swing on them,
A tourist
Might carve his name,

There are not many birches
Left these days .

And that's a crying shame.

Pollution might be killing
them,
Bugs might be drilling them.

Bird nests should be filling
them,

For I love them
Just the same.

Hemingway Skiing at Schurs

Choice or Chance
February 16, 2007

Gigantic gray rollers- with a
grudge-
Stratospheric, catastrophic
clouds- without- mercy
Edge slowly,
Now lurching towards Nubs.

Five-thirty golden sun
Gilds these atmospheric
monsters
Into appearing harmless
Or fun.

But, onward
Spill they, bedecked,
Belching,
Snorting, smothering our
deck.

With that terribly thick
Covering,
Called, "lake effect."

Ice anglers
Abandon their shacks.
Now swiftly make tracks!
For mainland safety
Avoiding the cracks.

"No fish is worth it!"
Most will remark,

-

But, Skiers rejoice,

"Hit the slopes before dark!"

Two totally divergent
Points of view.

Makes me wonder.
Does it you?

Some see a snow storm
And run from its blast,

While another group
Loves it,
Prays it will last.
In what camp can we find
you?
When challenges begin?
Do you gasp or do you grin?
Run you out
Or run you in?

Will you shrink?
When times get tough?

Be thee firm
And boldly adjust?

I think of the German
Para- glider girl-
Caught up by accident in
similar swirl,
Drifted into a terrific storm,
She did not panic, as would
be the norm,

But rode it out

Thirty thousand feet high,
Landed in Australia with
only a bruised thigh.

Or Lindberg,

Or Yeager

Sound Barrier Breakthrough
The Wright brothers too

-

What did they do?

All traveled beyond
the status quo

Danced on the edge
Of disaster for you!

Where would we be
Without (wo)men of vision?
Harnessing: air travel,
Nuclear fission,
-
Probing deeper than those
gone before!
Men of adventure,
Loving the lore!

Day Before Spring
(One Solitary Mink)
March 19, 2009

Twenty four most bleak
degrees
With bitter wind which rocks
pine trees
Leaves nothing to brag
about or sing
This blessed, last day
before spring.

Yet one solitary, slender
mink
With caution wends his
nervous way
Along the frigid brink
Where slippery flows an icy
ledge

With jitter, stops he brief at
River's icy edge.

Fleet of foot this furry friend
so fair,
Observed me long his jerky,
pensive bend.
Exposed is he to diving gull
or hawk or minion from the
air,

Yet, risk takes he!
His true love for to see.
Who nesting 'mongst these
craggy rocks a lee
Waits patient, hungry,

winsomely.

Then silence brakes as
witty, wily male
In gentle squeaks today
Her purring threshold
breaks,
His fur all sleek in auburn
-gray.
Both soon will dine a regal
way
On seaweed, snail and
crayfish tail.

Here's living testimony shrill
How Father's all-sustaining
will
Doth share
With modest critter donned
in finest hair.

Makes each of us most
vividly aware
Of Father's all-pervading
love and care,
Up-lifts creation's every
move,
Triumphant living to declare!

Simple living off the land
With food and lodging found
at hand,
Crustaceans, berries, grains
all dried,
All Providentially supplied.

I hope to meet again that
mink.
To thank him for his sermon
preached,
To share uncluttered goals
I've reached,
Enjoying first spring rains, I
think
much I've learned from that
fine mink.

Dust Devils
December 6, 2006

Dust devils in May
Called whirligigs in winter
Mindlessly scamper about
Stirring up trouble,
As they cut a surly swath
Of destruction
Across our placid,
little bay.

Canyons

Of empty stanchions
Shimmer
Where trip-less sailboats
used to ride
Offering their wave-made
rhythms
Of squeaks and thumps-
Unruly tuggings
'Gainst the unrelenting
Mooring lines of summer.

Like unruly child
Of a broken marriage,
Spoiled rotten
By mother's guilt,
Plays her to the hilt
And bone,
Suddenly(on a whim)
Severs the matriarchal
tether
Midst most inclement
weather,

Hops a bus
To nowhere,

Donned in costly mohair,
Longing for anywhere but
home.

Oh! the anguish of it all!
Will he ever call?

Acting out is not a life-
Destination only strife,
Of no use at all,
Like summer
Sun Devils
Or those pesky Winter
Whirligigs (just stirring up
trouble).

January Sunset
January 19, 2007

We have entered
Winter solstice.
Every day brings
Extra sunlight-
Brightening.

January skies
Show stratus-streaks-
Serious six-mile, purple
peaks
And pimples
Cresting Nub's pine tree
-dotted dimples-
Whitening.

Subtle strokes
Of mauve, and pink
Blend with neon

Orange, I think
All landscape artists
Would hang it up today,
then faint-
Defeated!

One can sense this time of
year (my dear)
Eternal rhythms
Which appear
As God, His twilight
Paints.
Repeated.

An upscale treasure
Mine revealed,
More than usual, sensual
pleasure.

One that touches
Deep within,
A spiritual,
Mystical,
Atmospheric festival,
Without earthly measure.

Slowly steamy mists
Enshroud our caustic cliffs,
Add drama with summation,
Reminding all
Just how it was
At Father's First Creation.

Gaze we at
His visual memo
Cosmic forces here do
demo
Awe and honor,
Adoration,
From His precious
Christian nation.

January Thaw
January 6, 2008

Exposed…in a sense
Having my blanky
Ripped off me,
Revealing my uncovered
innocence,

Just when I was
Getting friendly
With frigid temp.
Deep-wrapped in winter's
discontent,
Hypnotic, tense, in awe,

Like a thief, breaking the
law!
Then here you come
overnight
Like potato blight,
Like a fishbone caught
in my craw,
Here come you-
January thaw.

Ski resorts lament your
warm breeze
Stalled snow machines
Incessantly wheeze
In low Walloon wails,
"Look what you've done to
our manicured trails!"

"It's a freak, an anomaly!"
Weathermen scream,
"Just a kink in the
dominating jetstream.
'Gainst a southeastern high
Piling vapors high in
the sky
Pumping warm moist airs
Up from the gulf."

Like a wolf
Set loose
In a farmer's hen house,

Worse than a cheating
spouse.

But you've got me
Down on my knee
Pleading for our meager
economy

'Cause up north here

Where in winter
No one goes
UNLESS IT SNOWS...

Take this!
Right on the jaw!

You no good...
January thaw!

Life is Good in Petoskey
December 26, 2006

Gently roll yon purple hills.
To wit my faint heart often
thrills
At panoramic vista,
This fine day,
'Cross LT Bay.

Multi- shades of grey and
blue
Enhance my harbor-
widened view.

I cock my head to listen
As breakers crystallize
Lighthouse Point and
glisten.

Leave trillions of pirate
diamond gems
When mizzen mast is
missin.'

I strive,
I climb beige rocky bluffs

To block brisk breeze
Around bare cuffs,
Yet I heard my lungs a-
wheeze,
"Today,
I really feel alive!"

Army's gift from engineers
Break wall tends to calm all
fears
Making life in harbor town
most workably possible,
Bearable, livable.

This year surely had its'
thrills
Occasional valleys
but mostly hills
Yet, who's counting?
Who is there that tallies?

God's grace!
I do enjoy good health,
An artist's wealth,

But time (in stealth).
Creeps up my legs.
I've lived my life
I've quaffed his dregs.

All in all it does appear
In old P'Town

'Twas a very good year.

Without being risky,
Say life is good-
God is good-
In my dear town,
Petoskey!

'Mid Stark Sheets
January 28, 2007

'Mid stark sheets
Of snow and ice,
Pair of crow greets
Sunday's nice.
Wise are they
Which seek their prey
So frigid now
'Neath Winter's barren,
Frozen brow.

With one word
Their loving Lord
Supplies the bird
(Not luck)
And all within the flock.
Watch I now
For mirth or meaning
In their constant,
Nervous preening.

In this weather
Every feather
Gives them health
And needed stealth.
Swoop they down
On salted flyway,

Finding food
Along our highway.

Winter- weary squirrel
Or coon
Will fill his crop
Before it's noon.

Also we,
If we so dare,
Stare and study
Winter fare.
Find we grouse,
Precocious mouse
Or slower hare
Beyond his lair.

Our food is there
And all we wish.
Hole in ice
Will yield us fish.

Our loving Lord
Won't let us hoard,
For every day
As is his way…
"Give us this day

Our daily bread"
So He can have His say.

As is His deal
Each perfect meal
He doeth conceal
So trusting is The Way.
Faith
Within such simple acts

Creep in our lives
'Till they are facts.
Makes us give a nod.

Ask wily crow
For he doeth know,
Depends he,
Subsistantly-
Totally
Upon God

Wild, White and Worrisome
February 15, 2008

Lighthouse Point is heard
to ask-
While winters knurled
fingers grasp
Bluish tongues of lurid ice-
Wild, white and
worrisome-
L.T. Bay lies motionless,
Silent, stiff and flat of task-
"How long this Arctic
freeze?
I beg, Sir, send a southern
breeze-
Furtive, freeing, fast!"

Like mental states stuck in
the past
Wedged in ancient ways
of seeing-
Frigid, rigid ways of being-
Lost to limber's way of
walking,
Lost supportive, patterned,
talking.

Lonely are these Lenten
days-
Gone the fluid, waves of
gray,
Lest Cirrhosis find a stay,
Each hollow crust must
rend its prehistoric quay.

Stuck like legalistic
Pharisees-
Messiah's here! Yet blind
to see
The Law fulfilled-
Compassion thrills our
waking.

Pleasing Him consumes
our time,
Thawed by love, He lifts
our frame,
Melts the grip of fear
emotion,
Sin, now drowned in
deepest ocean!

God's Wintry Musical Landscape
January 22, 2007

(To be read with drama and wide range of feeling.
Meanwhile music from Schumann's 3 rd symphony movement
Larghissimo is playing in background.)

One great built-up bank
Of cumulus-nimbus-
Cloud of rank,
A packed-high storm
With winds now swarm
Off primrose Harbor's
shank.

Late PM sunlight
Brightens, lifts
And accents clouds
Winds recent tiffs
Much like upward jutting
Arizona buttes Or cliffs.

Wintry stratus start,
Puff up purple's raging
part
Yon gilded fluff
Yield regal stuff
With status
Now for God's
Late- evening- landscape-
Art.

Majestic!
Symphonic works aglow
With rose embellishment
below
Now lurks
Among bombastic breeze-

works,
Wind through weeds
Give voice like reeds
As Maestro heaves
His sacred Oratorio.

Darker gray
Now leads the fray
With classic fight
'Tween light and dark
While wood-winds speak
Through twigs that bark
To heighten passing
passions
Of the day.

Perfected tension (hours
away)
Sees night-time wrestling
Darling day,
LaMare brings in
Tomorrow's sin-
A plot
Protagonists often win.
Fast- moving blow
In vast array
With swift mosaic
movement,
Dump with trumps
Light snows that glow
A brassy tone

improvement.

With daylight slain
The willows swing,
Then sadly sing
This solo lilting, strained,
Vibrating, minor aire-

"Winter, Dear,"
God doth declare,
"Hath triumphed fare!
Will stay
And be
A month or three
Stow not thine special
underwear!"

Spring

"All you have to do is write one true sentence. Write the truest sentence that you know."
~ Ernest Hemingway

Another Way to Look at Weather
(I've made my peace with snow)
March 9, 2008

Trillions of tiny crystals
Flutter through my
evening sky,
Silent atmospheric
symbols
Of God's good love for
you and I.

This minute, mystic lace
Doth dance against my
rosy face
As if to geometric
measure
Or deliberately trace
The status of our human
race.

Curious, climatic
treasure
Doth reel, then dip and
flop
Much like a special
feather,
If finally to drop
Into a mental box
Which science coldly
calls...the weather?

But since my close
brush with death,
These later days I've
come to see
The wind
As God's infinitely loving
breath,

Our rain, His tears
Which do support,
sustain,
Grow crops, maintain
Our health and wealth
throughout eventful
years.

What we call snow,
I've learned to know,
(Yes, cheerfully
embrace)
As blessed comforters of
God's good Grace
Which draw us near in
fleece so horey
Through Christ,
To see again our
Eve-lost glory.

Day Before Mother's Day
May 9, 2009

Slate gray skies
Dominate our eyes
This day before Mother's
Day.

Moderate chop with
breeze
Captivate the seas
As God's emerging spring
eventually has her way.

Unusual flocks of
sidewinding swallows
Take wing. Quick-diving
fellows,
Dining on some mid-air
minions
Having very small
opinions.

Reminds me that our
Lord, in His way,
Is Mothering us all
Every day.
Winter through fall,
If we stop to see

His personal nurture
Ever present care
Make sure needs are met
For you and me.

Stop, look, see,
All the Mothering

That goes on.
Sharpen your wits.
Stop, look, feel,
A love so immense, so
rich, and real.

Unconditional, universal
It never quits.

Earthly Mothers point to
Him
Show us a shadow of
things to come,
If they are transformed
from within.

Open the Word to let Him
in.
Tell Bible stories
Let faith begin.

Nora did all this for me-
Started something she
could see
Sent me to a Christian
school
Even though it wasn't
cool.

Bless all Mothers in this
realm
Putting Father at the
helm.

Early Spring Blizzard
April 10, 2007

I'm not much of a
weather wizard
Can't help but take it
personal
That Winter had it in her
arsenal
To give us this early
spring blizzard!
I'll have you know
Kids were forced to roll
Easter eggs
Through six inches of
snow.
So, Mother nature, "Tell
me true,
Is it something that we
do,
That puts us in danger
Of getting all your
anger?"

"So help me, Nora!
Are we acting like
Sodom & Gomorrah
That causes you to
unleash
Four full days of vertical
sleets?"
I know my grandkids are
unruly
But your reprimand's
unduly-
Gale-force winds for one
whole week
Makes bones and

homes begin to creak!
Our robins were finally
back,
The lawns were nicely
turning green,
But snows like this
That you let go
Are most unmercifully
mean!

Forgive us for our many
sins,
Just let up on these
powerful winds!

Hail & snow as
punishment
During early spring is
tantamount
To feathers onto boiling
tar
For peeking in the
cookie jar!
It's too extreme, Nature
Dear!
Snow said, "adieu" for
another year!
Guess I'll never figure
out
Why you gave us such a
clout?

There's just one thing
that is amiss?
What did we do
To deserve all this?

Easter Sunday Morn
March 23, *2008*

Surreal, subtle blue
With grayish hue
Mists enshroud our quiet
bay today.
Ice anglers kneel (not
proud)
With patience say, "Tut,
tut
We worship in a different
way."

While lines of Christian
Pilgrims
Wend their way
Wind and sway
To church
On this High Holy Day.

Easter brings to mind
Our triumph o'er the
grave!
How every cell now wants
to say,
"Alleluia!
Halleluiah, Haaaalay
Luuuuueeeeyyaaaaa!"
Yet as we've seen
Not every tongue and
throat
Feels thrilled to shout
To sing, to dance
To jump about-
Rejoicing.
But for me, long ago today
Christ paid- our sins

atoned-
His resurrection paved the
way
For us to reach Eternal
Home!
Sins, death now have no
power, hey!

Victorious shouts
Across this bay
Are Myst'ry- Bourne
Misty echoed
On this Holy Easter
morn!
While Christ, Eternal
Angler, plies
Through ancient
augured holes
In skies,
Wrapping hooks of
steadfast love for bait,
Pulls like fish
All those who wait
To part these mists
With subtle rays
To melt a heart of late.
And thus, will start
A whole new phase
Of Higher Life
Across this transformed,
quiet bay.

And now he kneels
Not just for sport
Instead this angler
kneels to pray!

<u>Global Warring</u>
March 12, 2007

(In memory of Don and Shelly Paton's son killed in action in Iraq. Private First Class Justin T. Paton, 24, died Saturday, Feb. 17, 2007, in Balad, Iraq, from injuries sustained in Operation Iraqi Freedom..Justin was born on July 4, 1982, in Petoskey. Justin grew up in Indian River and graduated from Inland Lakes High School in 2000. He attended Northern Michigan University.)

Shrouded in Monday
morning weeping,
Yon rolling hills lie
grieving,
Bluish/gray adagios of
arched backs
Weep like Mother's
sealing wax.

Left ring finger of
Michigan lore
Lays in wait
For spring now late
While Allah plucks our
boys in war.

Terror tactics, nine-
eleven,
Hate's reward- a made-
up heaven,
"How long?" I hear her
moan,
"Before my boys come
home?"

Unfortunates return,
Without a leg,
An eye, an arm,
The question beg,

"What will it take
To end our global
warring?"

World police,
Misguided choice,
Always starts with
twisted voice
To bait our young
marines.

We've better things to do
These days.
There's pie to bake and
fruit to can,
Than blow ourselves to
smithereens.

Incessantly In Youth

April 5, 2008

Ice blackens now,
Sinks deeper down
below.
Appears gray solitary
angler,
Waist deep in river's
clear, cold mouth
Casting lures incessantly
in youth.

Persistent, patient rare
Determined is his fate.
Hooded invader plies his
craft,
Riveted, focused on
bobber small,
Sensing gentle nibbles
on his special bait.

Nudging upstream
Stealthy as you wish,
Whipping, thrusting,
thinking like a fish
Our boy ventures
Shallow waters to reveal
Absence of a fishing
creel.

From this surmise we
aught
His motives are for
sport-
No hungry mouths to fill
Simply here for the thrill.

Catch and release- a

noble motto
But mercury and PCB
Another ingestion "not
to."

Then river Bear
Begins to share:
"Youthful, too was I once
Home to grayling- two
hundred ounce,

Jumbo perch, exotic
trout,
Used to pounce, to
surface all about.
My current then
Was strong and wide.
Tribal foods did I
provide,

Then came the lumber!

Giant logs
Ripped my banks,
My fruitive bogs,
'Till now I barely
Reach the knee
Of youngsters such as
thee.

With many extinct
species gone
Never to be seen again
Tears now flow to honor
these
Progress left me little

gain.

Brushing by your loins
Gives me hope for more
to join
To tend my river special
needs
Kindle kind and gentle
deeds.

No more pollution,
please!
Toxic run off makes me
wheeze.
Unwanted trash
Give me a rash.

If more youngsters get

on track
Maybe rivers will come
back.

We are the blood stream
Of a nation.
Pollution and disregard
Could well mean our
termination."

Young angler gray
Will mark this day,
Will reach his many
peers.
River Bear must not
despair,
Belay his many fears.

Life Along the Bear
May 1, 2008

Ever so slowly now this
time of year
Poplars are budding a
rust colored tear
Inching out gradual bud
also the balsam
Testing the weather to
see if it's wholesome.

Bachelors buttons,
profusely all
Enjoying their purple
with white colored shawl.
Spread they outlandishly
just before night
To watch lady slippers
curl at the sight.

Just kicked a rock from
our trail,
Another makes two,
Might trip on these some
day,
You might too.

Cowslips are grazing
Like fine yellow cloth
As butterfly tastes them
Disguised as a moth.

Next to wild blackberries
Bluebells do dwell.
I judge by their primrose
They're doing quite well.

Now see we the willows
While approaching the
pier
These droopy limbed
flora
Enjoy living here.

Bear slides 'long all of
them,
Rapids now swirl,
As downstream
Male mallard
Just primps for his girl.

My spirit soon follows
Bears' run for the Lake
(Lake Michigan).
I spy salmon and
steelhead
As spawning they make.

The Bear-
Near Petoskey's brown
waterfall
Washes flora and fauna
Both large and small.

Bless'd town's
Bountiful bloodstream
Vital and pure
Keeping her healthy
Is our job for sure.

While fishing
Or walking
Her waters so dear,
Pick up that garbage
And discarded gear.

Each eco-gesture
We render so dear,
Ensures she will
Run clean
Another good year.

Noble Robin- Michigan's State Bird
May 1, 2008

It's a sure-fire fact,
A bonified sign of spring,
When one sights a robin
Fly north on his wing.

After sewing all winter,
(Then losing one's
bobbin),
I'll have you know,
'Tis thrill "Best of Show,"
Spotting my first robin!

Industrious they,
Busy all day,
Weaving their nest
From yesteryear's hay.

Making his bed,
Now hops on new grass,
Cocking of head as if
going to mass,

Listens he for his
favorite food,
Low angle worm fare
For his whole mottled
brood.

Deftly he pokes
Just after a nod
Tugs up a crawler
From Michigan sod.

I hear him "chirrup"
Often for rain.

Prays he to God
So to dig more worms
again.

But what I like best-
On a maple tree crest.
Just after that rain
(When I find my lost
bobbin)
He'll thrust his red breast
And thank God,
Will my Michigan robin.

One Solitary Pine
April 8, 2009

Perfectly proportioned,
Tapered, tall,
Growing steadily through
ten score fall.
But troubling.

Tender shoots of bluish
green
Reach upward eager to
be seen,
By long and lazy
summer sun.
Now doubling.

Lakefront breeze
Caressed like mother's
Moisturizing some
special needle leaves
Yet where are all the
others?

Perched high upon this
rocky bluff
Nutrients cannot be
enough
To sustain it's younger
progeny?
These queries rise of
mine
Just how this lone
stately pine has done so
exceedingly fine?

And then the answer
softly came

As clear as my own
worldly name
As barren as these rocks
may be
With nothing to support
a tree
Yet grows here one so
perfectly
It has to be from God!

While I pondered
pensively
What happened next
has made me frown
A man came by and with
gleaming ax deftly
chopped it down.

I tried in vain to halt the
ax
He reassured with these
plain facts,

A sculptor he while deep
in prayer
Had learned the
gracious Lord had
definitely led him here
To carve a cross for all
to see
Symbolic of his Son's
great love.
So now it all comes clear
to me,
The purpose of this

perfect tree.
It rests my heart and
weary mind

Why God would make
One solitary Pine.

God's Own Pin-ball
April 30, 2009

Have a seat this star-lit
night en mass.
Or lie upon
This bed of dew-kissed
grass
To contemplate our
transverse, all-
expanding universe.

Planets, galaxies, and
stars,
Do whirl, yet spin as far
away as Mars
Only to return again to
their respective home
Like some enormous
pin-ball game.

Travel they from darkest
space and sing
As shot from some
gigantic spring
But delicately balanced
each
Within respective
designated ring.

Set in motion with the
coin of God
The wizard of arcane

arcades
Beyond all time
As of earth, decades.

Then travel we
Upon this misty marble
blue
Eras, eons pressing
through
The vastness
insignificant and yet

The player knows us in
His special way
Waits for us to rise to
bounce
And roll through each
God-gifted day

(We) Designed by Him
To shine, to sing,
To chime and ring
To light up specials
Where it's dim

Science claims "The Big
Bang" notion
(A Big Bang) has set
these wondrous worlds
in motion

Some grandiose cosmic explosion

How impersonal!
How cold!
To relegate this intricate,
intelligent design so bold
To mere accident
To happenstance or
mindless, witless
whimsy!

Why just last night
My God informed their
theories are quite flimsy
Gave me a coin
To slide within
To whir to spin

My inner world begin

As above, so below
My life to show
His Cosmic sense of
humor.
God is the boss He runs
This game!
Big Bang a fleeting
rumor!

Triumphant victorious
Lives lead we
Granting grace for all-
expanding To see
Compassionate and
warm
Grand pinball we!

Spring Annoyance
May 14, 2009

Blankets of new
dandelion
In gay profusion lay.
Cover vast green
hillsides,
As nothing we could say.

Thick clouds of light gray
midge-lings,
Swarm as summer entry
nears.
Food for fish and bird
alike
Belaying hunger fears.

Walking into a flock so
dense
That one flew up my
hairy nose,
Then before I let a sigh
One flew in my lazy eye.

Mother Nature's spring
annoyance,
When Midges do their
mid-air dance.

Makes long strolls
through dewy grass,
Delayed until they finally

pass

Adventure waits
Along our bay,
For those with time to
find it.

But dodge today
The minute midge
I hope that you don't
mind it.

Spring At Last!
March 28, 2007

Lighthouse pier
Doth now appear
As a long- backed spring
lamb
Shedding winter wool.

The pull
Of each March ray
Tugs at six-month icy
growth
To melt
His shaggy, frigid pelt
As froth.

White bay ice recedes
To once again free
frozen waves
To flirt and frolic
With each playful, April
breeze.

This late March day
Must have it's way-
Six thirty sun with
eastern breeze
Has now begun to gently
squeeze
All ice out of LT Bay.

Watch, observe
Each graceful curve
Dissolve,
As sinful Winter
Slowly dies
From Spring's Eternal
love absolve.

Month eleven until now
Each frigid way
In due course grants a
day
To love's persistent vow.

Even Winter's hearty
fowl
Now nest
Then court to mate
As they do best
To chirp
If not to howl.

While in the dregs
They hatch their egg
Each screech so shrill
Beseech and thrill
A fledgling's life doth

beg.
Hear snickers
As stone pickers
(AKA fudgies or
stooped- over Petoskey
tourists)
Comb the thawing beach
To pocket home
Each rock- in- reach-
Small token which we
pay
To see them exit at the
end of day.

Spring at last!
Great God, Almighty!
Natives gasp!
Gone the long and icy
grip
Of frigid Winter's finger
tip,
Ah! Sweet kiss and
warm embrace
Of Spring…

At last!

Spring Mystery
April 8, 2005

Urged onward, ever
upstream,
Muscled bodies, silver
agleam,
Smelling birth bed, cool
serene,
Steelhead dreams of
coming home-
Spawn and die no more
to roam.
Deep mystery to me,
when I observe,
Timely cycles all
converge-
Weather, climate,
temperature-
All is perfect-every factor
Yet remains just one
detractor,

Could this all be
accident?
Primordial ooze each
incident?
Evolving zygote, smart
amoeba
Precocious protozoa-
sees-all?
Planned this one lazy
afternoon?
Come on now! I am no-
one's fool!
King and Coho ply this
pool.
Sockeye salmon, brown
and rainbow
Listening to their
Helmsman Able
Gifts from God for dinner
table!

<u>This Symphony Called Spring</u>
March 26, 2009

Ducks and geese of
honk and quack are
back.
Finch, wren and robin
also found their way.
Songsters all to thrill this
icy tract,
This silent winter land-
along- the- bay.
Throaty maestro's trill all
day
Perch bursting forth with
lilting lay,
Most thrilled to nest, to
mate, to gather food,
Enjoying God's fair world
so good.

Arpeggios pervade their
forest scene-
Free concerts of a
cherished theme
Find feathered chick-a-

dee and sparrow
(Pierce frigid, rigid inner
man)
Reach deep into one's
mystic marrow.
Rich, unique, grand
symphony
Our best of present
moment wealth,
Adagios most fleeting
ring,
Force auditory stealth.
Come savor these
mercurial days!
These musical motets
called March
Find nature's larks doth
spark "The Beast"
Where current springs,
Doth echo deep where
wisdom sings
Creating spirit health.

To Grow Up Protected
May 13, 2007

Low lying beaches-
Undisturbed estuaries
Shallow sanctuaries,
Best ponds for breeding
by
Crayfish, shellfish
Pollywog and fry.
Natural regions
Free from rough
Wave action,
Where young of each
specie
Manage to gradually
grow-
Develop protected and
secure.

A much needed
commodity
During that delicate
stage
Which is true at any age.

Natural seedbeds,
Free from stress
Where incubation can
take place,
Sheltered from intruder's
gaze-
Invasion-free.

Yet one demonic
species
Does exist-
Horrific at it seems-
Which raids it's own

God-designed SafeZone
Willie-nillie ripping,
Evicting,
Stripping!
To kill!
In order to sell
It's precious little parts

Legalized murder
To access it's stem cells
Political partners
With the healing arts.

They brazenly invade
The safety of their womb
Clipping unborns with a
surgeon's comb,
Barbaric specie-
Godless, Liberal woman!

Evil! Selfish!
Bad!
E'Gad!
Simple shellfish
Protect their growing
youth,
Even guppies
Hold them in their mouth!

But perversion has it's way
Inventing laws that can
They say.

'Tis sad commentary
On our day,

When the mundane
procreation act itself
Is worshiped
Yes, cherished, (as
sexual fulfillment)
While unborn product-
(IT"S A CHILD!)
Must be "harvested"
Or simply thrown away.

I speak
For humans yet unborn.
Those Blessed of ye
Whose Mother

Doth adore,
What she and Daddy
Loving does germinate
And never does she
Ever think to...
To play the whore,
To
Terminate!

If you are alive to read
this,
Then to you it truly is
A
Happy Mother's Day

When I Was Only Nine...
I Went to Heaven
May 20, 2007

Few can claim they've
been there
Few have seen those
pearly gates
Few have returned to
name-
Nor to recall what they
have heard
But I've been blessed
To give you same.

It happened fast
At a family outing-
One of the last
Along the banks of
Ocqueoc River
The thought of which still
makes me shiver

All my Boy Scout
cousins
Frolicked by the dozens
Unaware of river's tow
It was strong I'll have
you know
At only nine I still could
not float
Yet down stream I
began to slowly go

Dad yelled out,
"Where is Dave?"
"Blub blub," is all I gave,
As down, down, down I
sank.
Wallowing, swallowing
water brown and dank.

"Oh my God, Jesus, I'm
drowning!" I muttered.
Then I began to hear it
without fright,
Celestial violins- a
thousand fluttered
And like a magnet pulled
me upward
Through the tube of
light.

Peter was surprised to
see me-
"Hey, wait there son,
It's not your time!"
"Hasten on sir
I must see my Jesus!"
"Well go ahead, but the
faults not mine."
Further up the tube I
rose
Curious as ever
I struck a pose
For there He was.
My Jesus!

Now hear the ultimate
story
'Twas the grandest sight
yet
In black not white
As one would guess
For all I got was
silhouette
Due to his blinding glory

His thought tore through
my mind
Like a Mighty Wind.

"Son, what do thee with
thy life?"
A humble shrug of
shoulder
Was my lone reply.
In that moment flew I
back into
My waterlogged life.

Dad knew not how to
swim,
Yet prayed that angels
would deftly guide him.
Neck deep he reached
my grasping limbs
Which hugged his ample
midriff bulge.
Now praise the Lord that
I divulge
This unique hymn.
I have my loving pops to
thank.
As my weakened body
he caressed.
My chest he pressed in
hopes I'd pass
The river water that I
drank.

Gallons spat upon the
grounds
While my spirit made the
rounds
Reading aunt and uncle
thoughts of fear
mentally reassuring
each I was OK
what more could I say?

Fifty and six
Are the years
Since that ordeal
But today I feel
Compelled to share
Without any fears.

To drown is gentle I'd expect,
Peaceful, one just slips away.
However I must say,
To this day
I have a healthy respect
For Davey Jones' locker.

Learn to swim
As soon as ya' can.
Is my advice
Drowing's no way to see
Jesus' face.

He's nicely revealed
In the Good Book
Dive right in
Get into the swim
Of spiritual things
And thus fulfil your life.

Since that drowning incident.
What did I learn?
Learned I thus-
Our Heavenly father has a yearn
For friendship that is intimate

Understand, He's still

boss
But ever since Jesus
went to the cross
His redeeming death
Now paves the way
Like nothing else can
for close communion
'Tween God and men.

Stop and think
'Tis quite the thrill
Living waters we can drink
In a valley or on a hill
Our loving Father's there
Waiting to share
Every little spill.

This simplistic truth
I have learned since youth
None can compare
Anywhere on earth
The joy I share
Since my spiritual rebirth.

Your attention
Every moment-awareness
your affection
touched by His detailed Care-ing-ness.

Therefor ask [amours]
Ask him anything
In Jesus name
Believe that you have it
And it will surely be

yours.

We feel his presence
He is there for us
Night and day
Not a hair of us
Goes without His notice
His love is there in every
way.

Love Him?
Then love his children.
Try your best to
Serve the unfortunate
Which ever way you

can.

Hit the streets.
Help the needy.
Feed the poor.
Only preaching
When they're ready.

For in so doing
one yields His kingdom
With blessings upon
shelter home and
hearth;
Thus, bringing heaven
Down to earth.

You Found Me Worthy
April 3, 2006

In spite of
The ugly truth,
Acne scars,
One dead tooth,

Frightening marks
I've hid since birth,
Stretched out skin
Which meets my girth
(barely),

Arthritic joints
That hitch my gait,
Graying hair,
Receding pate,

Sagging breasts,
Baggy butt,
Polluted brains

Filled with smut.

Cirrhosis,
Psoriasis,
Rosacea, too,
Melanomas,
Proboscis blue…

Beyond all this,
As listed thus-
A week's worth
For air-of-brush,
And yet…

You found me worthy!

It takes a while
To find a file-
A category
In which to place

The transformation
That has taken place…

All due to the magnitude
of Your love.

I see You rise
Above the lands,
Nail-scarred feet,
Bloodied hands,

Out-stretched arms,
As if to say,
"Have you hugged like
me today?"

Please, Lord, make me
feel worthy!

I now see Grace
On every face,
Hold the judgment,
Ire in place,

For didn't you
Do the same?
For the leper
And the lame?

We're all your children,
Everyone.
All are equal,
Everyman!

Your blood-bought
Redemption Plan

Levels playing field
Like nothing can!

What joy!

Now fills my heart!
Now that I'm a part
Of Your Kingdom
Here on earth.

It took Your love—not
condemnation,
To see my worth and
every nation.

Be at peace all "ethnic
cleansers"
Calm all fear
And trepidation.

Feast on The Lamb,
Release the dove,
Look through the lenses
Of God's love,

For He who made all
things
Now gives our spirits
wings,

Has changed us
With His blood,
And now finds us all…

Worthy!

Summer

"There is no friend as loyal... as a book."
~ Ernest Hemingway

Advantage Catbird

Catbird's call
Reminds us all-
"Don't believe all the
sounds that occur."

What wails like a tabby
In a tree tall
We find covered with
feathers not fur!

How nature-ironic!
How terribly trompe
l'oeil. (French for fool the
eye)
How confusing for kitty-
This artifice (trickery)
ploy.

'Tis catbird's advantage-
Survive for a day-

Instead of becoming
A feline's filet.

God's sense of humor
Is certainly at work
He makes hungry kitty
Appear like a jerk.

Last night when I heard
it.
It made me turn twice.
I said, "Mother Nature…
That just isn't nice!"

So next time you hear
him,
Don't be surprised.
It's catbird declaring,
"I have survived!"

Another Million Dollar $unset
June 26, 2008

Ball of fiery light again
Framed by purple clouds
in flight,
Slowly now you drop
from sight
Into cold Lake Michigan.

Such radiance, my
Liege!
Sheer brilliance so rare.
As you shimmer this

summer's eve
Among my true love's
hair.

Orange now in your
twilight robe, so fare,
As gray clouds catch this
vaporous hue-
With all- encircling royal
blue.

Dreamers with empty
hands
Sigh for exotic lands,
But just cast me eyes on
One Petoskey horizon.

Patting mental purse.
Grandly enriched
beyond all verse,
Reminds me of the
million bucks

That I now "own."

Quite blessed am I in
ocular mindset
To have seen this
atmospheric tool-
This fleeting, gilded-
Midas jewel-
Another panoramic
Petoskey sunset.

Ballad of Donovan McGee
August 30, 2010

Birch bows violently
sway
Back and forth with
ease,
But troubled waters boil
in breeze-
In mystery today.

No small craft will ply
such seas-
To navigate, too brisk.
No captain worth his salt
would risk
A trip in such as these.

Alcohol or ignorance,
Would motivate a
chance.
No other urge
Would ply such surge
Unless… it were…
romance!

And so it was this
August three
To glide- to tempt- a
phantom fast
A love-struck captain off
did cast
His star-crossed love to
see.

Young heart,
headstrong, most
handsome man,
Proud Donovan McGee-
Star struck, one mind
now riveted
On nothing else but she-
His betrothed, his love,
his bride-to-be
Sweet, Molly Amelia
O'Shea.

Harbor Springs is not
that far,
One quick trip, if Don
owned a car,
But sailing there today
was nuts
Demanding skill and lots
of guts.

Yet jib he hoist,
His last wise choice
Took fate-doomed craft
Passed Lighthouse
Point.

But sheltered white-chop
Soon gave way
To Great Lake swells
Of high degree-
His bow rose high, took
daring dives, traversing
vast arrays.
Plunging deep each
tragic trough
Out-casting - Vee-
shaped sprays.

Swells fill his well
This side of hell
In sight of Moll' O'Shea.

Soon one last blast did
snap his mast,
Event he had not
planned.
Now, Don, sincere,
Began to fear
He'd ne'er again see
land!

Ah!... So, this day,
This troubled bay,
Did swallow his frail
craft,
That wave that crashed
into his aft
Did drown our fine
young nave!

Dark Specter raged for
three long days.
Did dine on Don McGee,
Yet, Molly scoured each
cluttered beach
Engaging all O'Sheas.

Yet somewhere a sun is
shining,
With seas of calm
serene.
Somewhere children
shouting,
Filled with childish glee,

Moll' has no joy, but
poutings
For fiancé McGee.
No fine regatta outings
From fashionable Harbor
Springs.

Now vacant stares
'cross L.T. Bay
Glare 'cross Donnie's
grave,
Her gossamer, long
white night clothes
Now catch each morbid

wave…

She made her peace
with Neptune
Felt drawn to pale
McGee
Brought end to this sad
nightmare
By joining him at sea!
Now each late summer
eve
Along Petoskey's sands.
Friends put aside their

cell-phones
Clasp tight each other's
hands
(To hear what each
might say)

They smell a mayhem
air,
Chilled winds disturb
each hair.
They reminisce of star-
crossed lovers…

Once lost on LT Bay.

Before the Fireworks
July 4, 2005

Mist hangs heavily
O'er Little Traverse Bay,
Softly cottons up to
Nub's,
Caresses Highlands,
Like a white cat's tail
Seeking affection from
these mountains.

Thousands of fudgies
(locals, too)
Mill about Bayfront Park
Searching for ideal spot
From which to view
The upcoming
spectacle.

Atmosphere is heavy,
dense,
Like Civil War

battlefields,
Waiting,
Anticipating
that first round of mortar.

My God!
What does this all
mean?
Are we worshiping war?
Do we …
Are we…
Worshiping war?

Do we need to relive that
horror?
Through fireworks?
The horror of it all!

Is this some sick
Vicarious, corporate

thrill?
Grim reminder of
Picket's ill-fated charge?

Petunias now intoxicate,
Mixed with smoke from
Sparklers,
Cigars and decomposing
fish carcass
Along the shore.

2.

Heavy air
Makes one aware
Of myriads of odors
That normally miss the
mind.

Like WW1 trenches
Filled with mustard gas!
Acrid reminder
Of a wicked war
In France.

Uncle Henry
Tried to fill me in (one
hunting season)
As he deftly cradled
His GI 30/40 Craig (or
was it his Springfield?
With frightening war
stories,
(Enough to fill my pants).

I lived through
WWII!
Remember the black-
outs,

Carnage counts,
Scrap iron drives,
Pulling my heavy red
wagon
Through alleys
In search of: pots and
pans,
Old R/R spikes.
Yikes!

Cousin Ted (Urban)
Stepped on a mine (in
France).
What's left of him
Came home in a box.
It could have been an
ox,
Or a dead horse,
We couldn't tell.
That war was hell!

Lived through Korea.
'Twas called a "conflict"-
Police action.
Hell, that was war!
No matter what
politicians tried to call it.

Brain matter
Was made to splatter.
Real bullets, bombs
Killed children,
Dads and Moms.

Screamin' Mimi
Just went up
Like Nazis threw at us.
Some mindless fools
Go,"OOH & AAH."

But, I recall it as it really
was-
Blood bath,
Guts every where!

Arms & legs shot off!
Body parts
With human hearts-
A-fly…
Pinwheels go up now,
"Lookie there,
A giant star fish!"

Don't I wish,
It could be
So antiseptic…

But I can't hold back,
"It's ACK ACK for

Wozniak! (Fred
Wozniak, best friend,
killed in flight over Nam)
Sky full of FLACK!
Bomber wings.
Terrible things!

Kids get their thrill,
But old folks know,
It's more than show…
These fireworks.

Another 4th slips
innocently by'
Yet have we learned
anything
As to why?
Why war?
Like, maybe…negotiate
Or something, already!

Coming of Age Without Knickers
September 6, 2010

Short pants were worn
By all little boys
When I was a boy
myself. (1940s)

As we grew up
And wore out our toys
Mom placed them on the
shelf.

Custom was then
To heave shorts; the
kicker
And make way for the
coveted teenage

knicker,

Older brother had a pair,
And so did Jimmy
Karsten.
No one heard of Vanity
Fair
Knickers were the
custom.

My hopes were high
That some day I
Would one day wear
them too

But they went out of
style
Through a shortage of
pile
Which we blamed on
World War Two.

So to this day
I'm bitter and quick to
bickers
For, alas, I never got
To wear my long-
awaited knickers.

But I know
Someday they will come
back
some stylist will see their
value

Or I will have to make
Some deals or dickers
So I can truly have my
knickers.

I guess it sends a deep
message.
Tis a rite of the male
passage
For boys who reach a
certain age

To shed the ranks
of boyish pants
Or forever live an
outcast in a rage
From my vantage point I
see
It embraces puberty.
One giant step toward
Manhood
To cast off infancy

Sure helps to ride a two-
wheel bike
without greasing up a
cuff

Guard the knee in roller
skates
Protecting from a nasty
scuff

Someday knickers will
return
The day for which I
yearn
And it won't take fancy
gems or pearls

Knickers will be found in
stores
The day they're sold to
girls!

D-Day
June 6, 2007

Times were different
then.
Each army had
uniforms.
Easy to recognize those-
Our foes
By the cut and color of
his clothes.

Battle Zones there were
Called front lines(as I
iterated).
We used all kinds
Of guns, tanks and
mines,
With little thanks
From The Franks
Whom we graciously
had liberated.

So then, guns, tanks,
planes, rocks
Ships, bombs,
Easily recognizable
frocks
Battle zones- never kids
or Moms,
Sad to say, fighting
lines-
Now all gone in these
strange times.

Now the enemy blends
in!
Nothing stands out!
Bombs are strapped

To girls and boys,
Who should be home
with their childish toys!

Now roadside bombs
Are set off by remote
Terrorizing Kids and
Moms!
Once they blew a hole
In the USS Cole.

A guy in a funny hat-
Named Yassar Arafat
Started this dastardly
Evil form of war.
Blowing up busses
Was his specialty.

His was a very cheap
shot
Killing boys
Asleep in their cot!
All Arabs should
Hang their heads in
shame.
For Arafat ruined their
somewhat-good name.
Still this day
And evermore
We bless the men
Of remember when-
Who died on Norman's
Shore-

Nameless lads,

Husbands, Dads
And our young sons-
Felled by ruthless Nazi
guns.

So wars have changed,
But not a tyrant's heart.
Who has not learned
That chaos, churned
within
Will fester there
And grow-
To stew and brew
Eventually to blow!

Right-wing clerics
Draw on this
Collective ire
To riot those
'Round race
Or lame sectarian fire.

See what they teach
From Ishmael preach
To slit the throats
Of Abram's rightful heirs.

Yet, they forget
That step-child (Ishmael)
met
To make his peace
As written on
The Holy Fleece.

But, scowls we stow
Down never-ending row,
'Neath Pearl white
markers-
Thousands lay,
Now catch the tears
'Neath sixty years
Of poppy growth,

Mute honor here today.

Highlands Hills ... Alive at Yom Kippur
September 17, 2007

Highlands Hills have
come alive-
A giant patchwork quilt
Where willowed pines
must strongly strive
For light 'neath olive
guilt-

Play paisley's game of
peek-a-boo,
Tucked in with fluffy

holsters
Painted mauve
From Mothers love
With matching festooned
bolsters.

Emerge a living
monument
To visions of Grant
Wood,
Adagios of dappled

yurts,
'Gainst Bed- framed
waves of good,

Neath never-ending,
froth-laced, skirts.
Beyond our coastal
ledge,
We hide here to avoid
the hurts
Of "walking 'long the
edge."

Beyond the sham,
Beyond the cries,
Beneath The Ledge on
lam-
God's undersea
Creation lies-
Primordial Pisces Land.

Here silent, grey
torpedoes roam.
And anglers dip with
thanks,
Invade these solid
muscled ranks
Who strongly smell their
"home."

Reluctant prophet,
Jonah, joined
These mystic banks
One year,
Rebellious, squirming
Twisting, turning-
Suva's Yom Kippur.

One day here, too,

We all must roam,
Deep- urged for sins
atone…
To join,
To blend within a town,

To find a space
Where sufferings end,
Alas! If just to drown,

Than serve a God who
Grinds our grist,
Who wants us give our
all,
To head His call,
To preach The Fall
And rise again in Christ!

Yet, perch we all
At Cross- roads tall!
If not to live or die!
We always flee the
Angler's Yawl
Who's pulling from the
sky.

But see the bait.
It is our fate,
His force will ne'er
abate!
Love pulls us now
And waits our vow-
Our inner clock can't
wait.

To take the plunge
Into the door
Obedient to His call,
To drop: "The lie

That makes us die"
A thousand times each
day,

I feel it yet!
My jaw is hooked!
I passed the test!
(This day I nest)
Within His all protecting

net.

My duty now is: Call the
Rest-
YES! Every living mortal-
To share the Plan
With girl and man,
To help them find the
portal.

My First Bike
June 29, 2008

When tricycles lose their
kid- allure
And nothing provides a
worthwhile cure (for a tyke)
Only one yearning is for
sure-
A kid must have a new, two-
wheel, bike.

Moms and Dads can't miss
this message.
So important! This rite of
passage-
That makes other kids to
stop and stare
Drooling at dazzling, new
hardware.

Shiny newness says it all
With handlebar streamers,
mud flaps call,
"Hey dudes, my parents
care
I'm all decked out. No mind

to share!"

When time came for my BIG
ONE,
I wondered, "Egad! Will I
have fun!"
Can't wait to see kid's eye
balls pop
As I cruise around the block
non-stop.

Then one strange, May Day
I heard Dad say,
"Your bike's tied to Mom's
rose bush
I'll walk behind to give a
push."

Right then I knew it was my
duty
To run and see this two-
wheeled beauty.

When what to my most

dubious surprise
I could not talk or believe
my eyes.
For there it was…a girls
bike and used! (That day!)
Plus poorly painted- Coast
Guard gray!

Oh, woe is me!

Self-image shattered,
depressed, self-scorned,
Not a word from God, nor
prophet- warned,
Never have I been so
burned!
Never have my guts so
churned!

How could they so have
missed the mark?
How I felt like Joan of Arc-
Bells rang in every steeple
Flame- licked at my fiery
stake
Misunderstood by my own
people…

And now…Ow! Martyred at
the age of eight!

What young, deep, ego
blows (today)
By loved ones… so they
say!
Who leave me now to face
the jeers.
Victimized now by three-
way leers:

It's used!
It's a girls!
And it's gray!

Now as I plow,
Through lengthy therapy,
While night sweats wait to
torment me,
My psyche warped since
only a kid
Deeply stabbed down to my
ID

I often ask,
"Life isn't fair!"
I ate my peas, ate my pear,
Cleaned my plate-(every
bite)
Said my prayers upon my
knees,
Just for this one, tiny task…
A NEW BOYS BIKE!

Was that too much to ask?

At age sixty- six, I say,
"What can I do for me
today?"
Since growing up can be so
fickle
And price of gas a real
pickle,
Think I'll buy… a new
bicycle!

What a grand discovery-
Taking charge of my
recovery!
Letting these cathartic

words today
Release the rage in this
small fray,

Thus lead me on my healthy
way.

<u>My Petoskey Stones</u>
September 18, 2007

Clear, cerulean waves will
roll.
Their tapered curl
Now pearl with wool
Then crash a-tumbly!
Clack! Then humbly
Hone...
This nondescript, grey
limestone.

Oh, genteel gem-
My state's fair rock
You're found
Around my cities blocks
Remnants of a coral
stand-
Destined soon to end up
sand!

Therefore; must we pluck
and savor,
Treasure proudly, show a
neighbor,
Souvenir from another age
Memories this city- saved.

Grand testimony mute!
Much more than visual
cute,
These rocks reveal a

bounteous sea, uniquely
Now as land.
Once teamed abundant-
thrivingly-
Tremendous coral strand!

These festooned fossil's
Frozen sleep,
Doth hold
Ten thousand epoch-
deep
Years, captured in its
hexic fold
Huge, strange, reptilian
registry.

Much larger than the
governor's house,
They roamed this
threatening crust to joust
Our fearful, cave- bound
ancestry.

Fantastic find, Ecstatic!
Along Petoskey's
Pleistician shore-
Where a fertile mind,
Dramatic!
Might conger pre-historic
war.

123

But, glaciers finally freeze
the fight
With mammoth- flavored
squeeze so tight-
Crushed history into vast
congeal,
Then time made rock we
mine for steel-
Called-
Calcium carbonite.

Admire now and honor
here,
More than ruby or
sapphire,
Museum mummy bones,
What crashing, tumbling
waves roll in
All Michigan, holds dear.

Knowing this, I'd truly
trade:
My flawless arrow head,
That trilobite beneath my
bed,
My Grandma's handmade
scones,

If once more I could hear
me bade,
In kneecap slap discover
made,
"Come quickly! Look, here
Mom and Dad!

Come see! Come see!
I've finally found
...Those precious
Petoskey stones!"

Bend the back to touch a
few.
Give them light,
Wash them through.
Stash in a velvet pocket.
Carry to Jeff's jewelry
store (Morning Star),
Fashion in a locket.

Now as I hold it high to
see
My childhood all comes
back to me-
My native land,
The city band,
Voices fresh as friends
condone,

Capsuled- keep like aging
tears,
Dangled meaning, heart-
enthroned,
Locked-deep a new ten-
thousand years,
Cherished memories I
have known,

Forever summer, sealed
within...
My Own Petoskey stone!

Now Bloom The Lilacs
June 4, 2004

Now bloom the lilacs,
Some purple, some
white,
Now fearless, unworried
Of frost in the night.

Thick clusters,
Tight bunches,
Like lusciously perfumed
grapes.
Emitting thick fragrance
These olfactory vagrants
With odor that clings to
my drapes.

Their heady aroma

Now fills my head
strong,
As my love plucks my
heart-strings
"Till they spring into
song.

Yes, today I surrender
To lilac and love.
Together they fit
Like a hand in its glove.

Gone is the anger,
The stress and its fears
It's only these lilacs,
My hand in my dears!

One Misty Morning
September 13, 2006

Early morning mist
(Like atmospheric
molasses)
Slinks, ever so slowly,
Into Little Traverse Bay,
In its own bashful way;
As if it doesn't want
Us to know we're being
kissed.

Like long-necked crane-
Long-standing, rapier-
beak wonder
Who eyes the sleeping

bay,
Knee deep in liquid
crystal,
Waiting for the slightest
blunder
Of silver wiggle to
wander
Within range...then,
Ah! Breakfast!

Gull, goose, in dining
mood,
Duck, tern and their
brood

Nervously wait, shore-
bound dears,
Patient for thick skies to
clear
So they too can search
their food.

Reminds me of creation
days
While earth and sky lay
in similar haze
Wait, as God made up
His mind
To mold some clay-
On such a day-
To shape mankind!

Why did He plan
To showcase man?
Give him glory
In this story?
While every other kind
All intertwine
On Emerald web-
Our matrix fine.

Yet, sustainability these
days
Has become a
meaningless phrase,
For who would guess

Or even think
That carrier pigeons
would become extinct!
And who was last to lay
eyes upon
Our majestic Western
bison?

"Grandma, no, your eyes
aren't failing
Never will you see a
grayling!"

Over-kill!
If you will,
Victims of man's gluttony
With species ending
every day,
The never-ending litany!

But pull away the misty
valance
Let emerge the tricky
balance
That we find ourselves
within today.
Food chain causes us to
think'
"Dare I eat the missing
link?"
Which holds these
strands
As only God can
understand?

It's all a test!
He did in jest
To cause us to tread
gently,
Abandon envy, greed
and lust
To foster inter- species
trust
So all can live
confidently.

God's plan for us is

wise-
Charging earth and seas
and skies

To live in harmony,
His grand and glorious
symphony.

The Sea Draws Me Today
August 16, 2006

The sea
Draws me
Today.

Is it the mighty mix
Of colors?
Or
The way it behaves?

Majestic rolling
Aquamarine,
With powerful
White-cap waves.

My raves
I place
On swells of Grace,
On liquid languish
'Gainst my face.

As warm
Sou'westers
Boil the bay,
They roust
My Spirits up
Today.

"Three-foot chop
Makes craft to hop

And skip along,"
I'd say.

While close to shore
An amber store
Of writhing foam
appears,

Crashing rollers
Smash the rocks
And spank
The piers,
As they always have
For many years,

But…never did
I notice it,
Like I do
Today!

Let me inhale
This minute!
Then… fill my lungs
To capacity!

God bless
Lake Michigan,
And
Also bless, Petoskey!

So Beautiful I Can Taste It
June 16, 2007

Misty, magnificent digits
lay
Snuggled fingers of fertility
Reach out triumphantly
Into tranquil LT Bay.

Cool, hazy languid, nights
With long lazy afternoons
Have burst trillions of pink
blossoms,
(like miniature balloons)

On the face of God's
green earth, I say,
There is nothing more
pleasing
To the eye
Than what we observe
this delicious day
Under a berry-magnificent,
Michigan sky.

As this famous fruit
matures,
When Mother bakes her
sweet preserves
And pies,
What once pleased the
eyes
Will treat the taste buds
too-
Its tartness tantalize our
eager, gastric brew.

In some sense one could
say,
"We actually get to eat this
day.
Eventually, if we have our
way,
To savor these conditions
as scrumptious pie or
cake."

As I glance
This cherry greenery,
Just can't wait
To "eat some scenery."

Don't mean to brag or
boast,
But might actually
Eat my way
All along our western
coast.
This observation we all
must make-
"If life is but a downstream
dream
I never want to 'wake.'"

Southern Breeze
September 2, 2007

Lord's Day Morn
O'er 'Toskey's algaed
shore
Where skies of robin egg
Meet tardy summer mist
Near Harbor's wispy,
mossy door,

A solemn southern
breeze
Lifts browning leaves
With ease
From sleeping trees
And fills great bashful
spinnakers
With submerged
memories.

Up north a farmer
Looks for these.
They bring warm days
With tepid eves,
Just what a fruit tree
needs.

But a southern breeze
rocks cargo
Of naive sailing craft.
Crashing swells
Hit prow to aft
Stir unrest from Chicago.

On such as these,
If left to vent,
Plant seeds of urban
discontent.

Catch they within one's
fibers claw
Snag they in one's
repressed craw
Like burr dock in the
chaps,
Seaports have this tragic
flaw

Big city smells
With rage attached
Big city ways
Where civility has
snapped.

This southern breeze
Lifts up the leaves
Of time,
Exposing secrets hidden
there
Fementing maybe, yet
sublime
A tale to seize
A feeling freeze
Fond memories of mine.
Flashback to countless
shattered glassen
shards
Benign neglect
Not fear I'd say
Clutter a past
Of old school yards.

My trollies hauled

This cramp'ed crew
Up bustling Belmont
Avenue.

Bounced their half fare,
kinky hair
Mid dust and gel afume,
Smelled sauerkrauted,
hotdog fare
Within this musty plume.
Twas our continual
carnival...
Twas carefree, River
View.

Thank thee, Dear Lord,
I've left this hoard
Of asphalt dwellers
Far behind,
But steaming aqua-days
like these
With swelling seas
Midst lifting leaves
In sudden shift of wind,

Still seems to bring them
rolling in,
Wafting thin as they
creep in,
Upon a southern breeze.

Stone Skippers
August 3, 2006

There's quite a science
Behind it all,
More than just like
Throwing a ball,

Skipping stones
Is not a lark.
Hear me out,
It's quite the Art!

Like a good ballet,
Light opera even,
When you're
Skipping six or seven,
Times across
A placid,
Wave- less L.T.Bay!

When a lad
Can get passed seven,
Spirits lift him on,
T'ward eleven!

As he skips on,
Passed eleven,
Found round flat rocks,
Seem sent from Heaven!

"I'm in the zone!"
Yips Todd or Kevin.
"It's in the wrist,
Or elbow even!"

"Snap of arm,
On surface tension,
Bend the bod,

Get full extension!

Then let 'er fly!"
They all say,
But I know there'll
Come a day,
When watching,
Is the only way,
That I'll enjoy
My skipping, latter day.

But, I must say,
Skippers today,
Seem so blase,
Though once,
They all were avid.

To tell the truth
God loved such a youth,
You might remember,
David?
Stone skipper supreme!

I'm sure it seemed,
A beautiful thing,
To see him switch
To leather sling!

Yet, face-to-face with
mean Goliath,
Must 've taken
Tons of faith!

But, David, knew
His stone's trajectory
And trusting, God,
Impeccably,

Deftly hurled
That fateful "mystery!"
Which sealed his name ,
Throughout all history.

Now every, "David,"
That is born,
Hunkers down,
To take his turn,

At skipping stones,
(And later sling-
It's a David thing)
And tries to learn
His place in time,
Just as I have done with
mine.

Summer Never Came
Summer 2004

With spring being late,
One could anticipate,
That summer,
Would surely be a
hummer.

Not so!
Oh, the shock of it all!
When July slipped by,
And farmer's reply
Was, "Sweetcorn? Wait
'till fall."

Teens still dive off light
house point,
But my pinky toe,
Will never know,

A frolic in
Lake Michigan.

Am I depressed?
Well I guess.
My back ole' Sol
Has not caressed.

Fish migration
Keeps a nation
Of our Redman
From starvation,

But; somehow…
I feel cheated!
Summer never repeated!
Pardon my non-oblation.

Unseen Hands
August 9, 2006

Just a sudden shift in
wind,
Lets it all begin-

Surface waters race
To other side of trace,

Land that's now be-
diked,
Is lunch; as well as,
Breeding ground
For fowl
And clam alike.

Life can be so fragile,
Yet nature counters,
agile,
Matching each anomaly,
Adjusting just enough
To raise a little family.

Looking closer at the
mud,
Reveals abundant algae,
food
For microbe world so

small.

Subtle shifts
On Earth
May vary,
Yet His watchful
Eye will tarry,
Causing unseen hands

To carry…
ALL OF US!

His strong hands won't
let us fall!
See how, God,
Takes care of all!

Water People
July 9, 2008

Never considered it
before. (Like eating
cake.)
Always; as long as I can
recall
Have found myself living
near a river or a lake.

Cannot picture me
anywhere else.
Water people, to me,
have more sauce.
Their minds behave like
the horizon-
A vast, expansive fluid
glide
Open for ideas creative,
winsome, and wide to
collide!

Trite to say, I know,
They seem content to go
with the flow
More patient (for
instance).

Like a good swimmer
going for a long
distance.

One slides into a
comfortable pace
If too fast out the gate he
could lose the race.
But water is the big
teacher- water is why.
Water I think
Trains us to fly-
Float, slide, glide... the
things
Arms and legs being our
"wings."

Don't mean to gloat
But most serious water
people I believe
Could probably build a
boat.

Fluid dynamics design
gets sucked into their

fluidity, watery, minds
Forming a structure a
sliding of the wind
No formal training just
hearing the raves
Feeling their vision cut
through the waves.

Water people easily
know how to dance
Will float around nicely if
given a chance
Bobbing and weaving
them doing The Dip.
Naturally knowing just
when to flip.

When trouble arrives
flow around it they.
When obstacles come
blow over (some way)
Like a flash flood or
tsunami of power.

A true water person
Would never consider
Leaving his lake or
favorite river.
Desert dwelling no
matter the reason
Builds a strong case for
regional treason.

Ask any real estate
agent these days
They'll tell you a house
on water really pays
But don't query a person
who dwells there.

(S)he'll be waist deep in
water
Shampooing his or her
luxurious hair.

Moses, Jesus, Peter,
fish, ducks, house boats.

Moses watched God
part the Red Sea
Think about Moses
whose life was saved
A river saved him but
'twas a close shave.
And Jesus began his
ministry in the Jordan
baptized- a royal
dunking
Then on the sea he went
walking.
Peter joined Him at
water walking too.
Surface tension seemed
to hold him
But lack of faith made
him fall through.

I remember my first
Esther Williams flick.
This gal just wanted to
swim (nothing else
mattered.)
And if left out of water
she might probably get
sick.

The Olympic divers and
swimmers
Cut through the liquid

with nary a glimmer
Rising triumphant like
nobody's fool
Knifing victorious from
the Olympic sized pool.
Water people are just
cool.

Think of the great water
people of all time

Many were relatives,
yours and mine.
Take notice next time
you see one or two
You'll take me serious
and say this is true.
"There's something
special about water
And water people too."

Autumn

"There is nothing to writing. All you do is sit down at a typewriter and bleed." ~ Ernest Hemingway

<u>Afternoon Along Old Tannery Creek</u>
November 8, 2010

Chattering brook,
Expansive look
Along a bright blue
L.T.Bay

Well-worn path
Adjacent bog
Near love-lorn log
Still moist from morning
dew.

Most leaves are gone.
Clutter the ground.
Soft breeze cools a

wrinkled brow.

Bed of grass
Where we relaxed

Stretched out
In summers past.
Spruce and cedar
Intoxicate our air,
Enliven your flowing
raven hair.

Ah... dear, fond reverie,
Of young-love days,

Of you and me
Among these gawking
trees.

Feathered touch on
tapered waist,
Of baited breath
On neck and face
While feeling free.

Unfettered from:
Your Mother's stare,
Father's louder, bolder
glare.

Unbridled enthusiasm
was us I'd say,
Adagio of adult dare,

A symphony of matching
moves
Conducted by pubescent
flair.
Days of deep
expression,
Free from gnawing fear.
Days of deep conviction,
Spurred by dauntless
care.
Days where etched
enchantment
Meet me everywhere.
Stay with me for a
lifetime
Which grand-kids now
will share.

All The Leaves Are Gone
October 19, 2006

All the leaves are gone
Dropped from branches
Everyone,
Not one stem remains.

Just like my friends from
school:
All have sung their last
refrains!

Yesterday we saw his
smile,
Today we buried, Billy
Kile,

But, Bill, is not alone,
He's interred with Ed
LaLonde.

Death calls not only fella
Remember(he also got)
MaryLou Centella
(Night before
graduation)!

We had our fun
In the sun-
Bright and colorful, I
would say,
But that was another
day.

Today we're stiff and
brown,
Stacked in neat, long
rows
At edge of town.
Just like Autumn
leaves…
We all are gone,

But our songs will linger
on:
"Rock Around the
Clock,"
"Peggie Sue,"
"Rag Mop,"
"I'm walking Behind
You,"

"Let's go to the Hop,"
"A Guy is a Guy,"
"Smoke Gets In Your
Eyes
"Mocking Bird Hill,"
"I Found My Thrill"

"Vaya Con dios!"
Ain't That a Shame
It's all In the Game!"

An Off-shore Breeze
November 21, 2006

{In memory of that fateful day on November 18, 1958 when The SS Carl D. Bradley sunk in rough seas off Gull Island near Beaver Island, MI}

An off-shore breeze
Like unfinished dreams
Blows away moisture,
Or so it seems…

And leaves eyes in the cold
(Or so I am told).

But today,
I must say,
It reminds me that I'm old.

Every joint a-aching,
Lower back a-quaking,
Guts ever- growling
To match the ever-howling,
Lung-challenged wheeze,
Of this off-shore menace-
With heart-stopping cadence-
This mind-numbing…
Off- shore breeze!

Early this morning
I checked on the weather,
Lengthened my tether,

Ignored every warning,
Crawled down bay front shores to see.

I saw Ghost Lady,
clopping,
Come from her shopping
Windbreaker flopping
Leaning now,
Bent at the knee.

Gulls that aren't gone
Are hugging the ground
As families of coots
Dine tugging at roots-
From seaweed we don't usually see.

So says my daughter,
"It blows surface water,
(Among other things)
Clear across bay
To warm Harbor Springs."

Just out of habit
I screamed, "Let them have it!"
And focused on Internal Pings.

Comes now an Eternal
Surging,
Not from none of my
urging,
Comes born on this
omen,
This threatening yeoman
This unwelcome…
off-shore breeze!

This blowing madly
Once took, The Bradley,
The infamous, Carl D.

Broke her in half
From bow to her aft
And plunged 'er
Deep 'neath Michigan's
seas.

Davey Jones wanted
To claim thirty-five,
Yet, somehow, two were
still alive-
Fleming and Mays, to a
raft did cling.
Rescuers called it a
miraculous thing!

God spared two that
bone-chilling night
While all around was an
unholy fright!

They shared their tale,
How their shipmates did
flail,
Gasp to breathe,

And eventually freeze.
But I know it all started
In lore yet uncharted!
It started with this off-
shore breeze!

Captain Bryan, in charge
of their lives that day,
Should've pulled into old
Green Bay.
But with no mind for ship
And ignoring the crew
He pushed that
"precious" iron ore
through.
Even Sturgeon Bay, was
a good place to sit tight,
But, Roland, ignored it
all that rough night.
Was it pride or
ignorance or alcohol
That allowed death to
take such a grizzly toll?

For the signs were all
there:
Pressure of air
Fell far 'neath the
"threes,"
Forty foot waves
snapped lakeside trees,
Rheumatics told him
deep in his knees,
As iced up lungs began
to wheeze...

Yet, somehow he
missed it, easy as you
please-

That oh! So, ominous
sign of the seas,
It felt so bone- numbing
He should've seen it
coming
On that ever appalling
off-shore breeze.

Now my cousins and
friends
Met unhappy ends.
My school -chums and
mates
Met ice-watery fates,
From terrible November
gales such as these.

I stand here pale
With this terrible tale.

(Don't want to be flip
As they watched her
bow dip)
For I could've sailed,
that once proud ship
While one fading eye still
sees.

'Twas a sad report
I tremble to retort
'Twas a November
I'll always remember,
There was no warning.
Just like this morning,
Only this ominous,
ghastly,
(Which I respect vastly),
Only this...nasty
Off-shore breeze!

Autumn Day Along the Warf
October 14, 2004

Seagull droppings
everywhere,
Fish blood puddles fill the
air,
Leave acrid testament to
anglers
Without a care.

Discarded Old Gold filter'd
butts,
Decomposing salmon eggs
Add their aromat' delight
To, an otherwise, gorgeous,
sight.

Liver spots on back of hand,
Beer gut straining every
gland-
Reminders of my sedentary
Life along the wharf.

Crewmen row in their
collection
Of summer's buoys
Leaving fall and winter free
To enter in from all
direction.

Lighthouse stands; as if to
say'
"Can't haul me in today,
Ask your boss for higher
pay.
Sentinel Tall is here to
stay!"

High-boomed dredge'
Hydraulic sledge
Adds romantic touch
To boat ramp ledge.

Love has blinded you from
this.
Eyes-a-flutter, postured
kiss,
Farm girl finds herself in
bliss
As we stroll along the wharf.

See the smells, hear the
lights
Senses skewed, exotic
nights
Reverberate within her brain
As I stroke her wind-blown
mane.

Tackle boxes all a-clutter
Boys and girls without a
mother
Make the best and often
wish
That Daddy did not "have to
fish!"

Bridge and break-wall filled
with anglers,
Frenzied hooks snag
neighbor's anger,
Yet, her inner peace

prevails
'Mid the turmoil on the
wharf.

Now, I too am deaf to
Hades-
Old men worshiping
Mercedes
Hobble past with arm in
lady's,
Fly I to my weathered
boards.

In my refuge she will find
me.
Peace and quiet will unwind
me,
As she feeds me wine,
Along the wharf.

Could it be her bovine diet
Keeps her calm among the
riot?
Pastoral patterns lead
Her measured steps today.

Does she harbor
Thoughts of: Mother?
Quilting patches for her
brother,
Silent sufferer in the
boondocks.

Not at all impressed with
moon rocks.

Does her lack of stimulation
Give her rights for mild
oblation
As she thrills at
Life along the wharf?

Will she yearn
For her return
To silo, barn
And pungent stanchion?

Will the pull of my dwarf
mansion
Perched atop the Gaslight
action
Still her mind from thinking,
"pasture!"
Fix sandals here, instead of
roam for home?

Queries rising, I'm
surmising
Pass like waves beneath
these docks,
As her new life here
unlocks.
Catch us innocently walk...
along the wharf.

Bernie's Last Fish
Oct. 24, 2010

But for God's Grace
Goes Bernie Malkowitz,
Cankle deep in
emptiness,
Pricy rod,
Premium reel,
Very expensive empty
creel.

Rain's supposed
To make fish swarm,
But not this lifeless
Sunday morn.
Bern shuffles toward his
blurring truck
Silence...cursing his bad
luck.

Thinks he also not too
far
Of arteries filled with
blood like tar,
Of heart a-pumping way
too fast,
Cardio-ic valve aghast-
His final fishing trip is
cast!

Bern recalls that look he
got
While landing that last
rainbow trout,
It's bulging eyes that
dared to haunt
To cast a spell- an omen
taunt-
Nightmare hooked he
one so gaunt!

Bern never made it
home that morn.
We found him slumped
behind the wheel
Entangled in his rod and
reel
His heart gave out when
blood congealed
Left lonely near that
empty creel.

Bern's widow had a yard
sale, drear-
Attempt to sell old
Bernie's gear-
But folks around
These parts all feel,
Bad luck comes from a
dead man's reel.

Big Rock Falls
October 21, 2004

{*Author's Note: In view of the fact that the U.S. consumes
more oil and natural resources than any other country on earth,
we are contributing to our own demise unless we come up with
viable alternatives for fuel other than
nuclear power plants.}

Mute Lake Michigan
licks her shores,
Once proud nuke gives
up her stores
Of hazardous waste(now
"out of range")-
Testament of times and
change.

Replacing coal, it had it's
glory.
Hippies warned, "Her
bitter story!"
How could pot-heads,
short of brain cells
Move the suits to ponder
future ills?

Just a stone's throw
from our shore line!
One slight error by a
crewman,
Be he, Homer, Alfred
Newman,
On a lark,
We'd all be glowing in
the dark!

Three-mile Island, noble
Chernobyl-

Good examples of their
folly,
Blew us all right off our
trolly-
Graves, mutations,
spreading cancer-
URANIUM! Now there's
your "answer!"

We got lucky, whew!
'Tis a fact, she never
blew!
Money wasted won't
renew
Tax-payer's squandered
dollar.
Harness hydro, air
power collar!

Let's go solar? What's
the harm?
Windmills once helped
every farm.
Was that simple E
solution
Too unscientific?
Without pollution?

Complicate our tranquil

scene?
Goldberg gadgets praise
machine.
Pardon my non-oblation.
Frozen toes give no
ovation.

If I could start burning
wood,
What's the harm to
ozone layer?
Plug the "gap,"
With Saran Wrap,
Madam Tupper surely
could.

Now rogue nations want
"The Bomb."
Give one last kiss to
dear old Mom.

Iran, Iraq, 'tis yet
unclear,
Why they would go
nuclear?
Perched atop vast
desert oil?
Somethin' isn't up to
Hoyle!

Why blame them for
nuke construction?
When we're The
weapons of mass
destruction!
As Pogo Possum did
discuss, *
"We've met the enemy…
and
He is us!"

The Boar's Nest

Of Old Boar's Nest,
Fred says,
"None's left.
Not a bit remains!"

But I retort,
"Oh, guess again,
There's memories my
man."

That old deer camp and
my deer blind
Was fine as I recall
Ken/Dew Hunt Club,

et.all.
Be firmly etched
In my young, fertile
mind.

I believe it was her
massive log
Their size and rough-
hewn edge-
Lingers on my mind's
-eye –ledge
Like Tip our family dog.

Pines huge no more are

found, I guessed
They're felled and
hauled away,
Like my big Dad and his
rough way
To their eternal rest.

Yet, many a deer hunt
Filled our lives, I'd say.
A lot got drunk,
Played cards 'till crack of
day.

But somehow due to
instinct
They always bagged a
crop.
Mom fried them each
their breakfast
When crews came home
with Pop.

(Fondly I recall) Uncle
Mac's bow legged boots
Laced tightly to the
knee.
Dad's hen-pecked
brother, Henry D,
When Laura turned him
loose.
(What smiles we all
would see).
Stan Klino and his Dad,
Bill Havel and Sonny
Boy(Schroeder)
Best friends who outwit
white tail's ploy

One team that hunts in
joy.

They crossed the crusty
Ocqueoc
Through willows with no
name,
We built Dad's blind of
rustic stock
None ever measured
same.

Those are my happy
hunting grounds
Filed deep in reverie
Now still that curious, old
hunt club
Remains a part me.

But, aged too
I sift through
For clues we partied
there
A rusty hinge,
A whiskey jug,
Some aged white tail
hair.

Alas, ah no,
My eyes can't bear
This loss of curio.

But memories linger long
And strong
Despite Fred's dismal
song.

Coming Out of the Fog
November 9, 2010

Great banks of thick
morning fog
Hang over and hide
Harbor Springs,
As fluffy packing
material
Ready to ship or
preserve for winter
storage.

Steady north wind
Exhausts itself
Seemingly unable to
clear-
Unable to let us have a
glimpse
Of the unique rows of
mansions
Stacked tightly along the
coast-
Like bundles of
expensive high-end
chord wood.

My mansion would have
acreage surrounding,
room to breathe, to flex,
To spread out,
With privacy, a high wall,

Complete with an iron
gate...
Like Graceland
(That Elvis knew how to
live)

Sun rises higher now
Slowly burning off some
of the vaporous
Wrap 'round the town
across the bay.

Two purple mounds
presently appear
through the white
atmospheric cotton.
Nubs and Highlands
peak through,
Leaving what looks like
a white angora cat
curled around the
village.

Purring sounds of rush-
hour traffic
Just add an eerie note
To that intrepid mist
which still remains.

<u>Dueltgen's Wood</u>
October 17, 2007

New as foam
Drying on these cliffs,
Old as rocks,
Which echo evening's
song,

Steadfast! These ancient
memories long,
Of our first kiss
In Dueltgen's Wood
With cedar odor strong.

They cling to trees

Like ag`ed moss

As part of you and me.
They are the taste
Of Boz's fries
To Cozy Corner haste.

Decades five
Have now sped by,
Left aged frames
In search of spry

Yet, lonely limbs

Will thrill
From once more your
embrace,
As deformed fingers
trace
That special smile
across your face.

My heart would race-
Leap from my chest,
Where cherished
Is the thought of
seeing... thee.

That pair of swans
Doeth bill and coo
Close wander `cross the
bay,
Their courtships now
know nothing
Of our love... back in the
day.

We wrestled in the
leaves,
Frolicked in the surf,
Laughed beneath these
giant trees-
Had greatest times on
earth.

Then cold war caught
us,
Led us separate ways.
You went into nursing. I
built rocket ships.
Surviving under
pressure
Learning NASA's ways.

Russia threw up Sputnik,
Put us all to shame.
But we caught up
With Mercury
Now in the hall of fame.

Neglect of vital spirit
Made me make some
slips.
I took a dive.
Forgot to thrive.
My rudder could not
steer it.

But in God's grace
I made this place,
Not too worse for wear.

I've gained some weight,
Got all my teeth,
Some thinning of the
hair.
I've slowed my pace
Endured the race
Yet miss you every day.

Am now retired.
Enjoy the days
Not hassled by the
union.
Look forward now
To eating crow
At our 50th reunion.

How empty life, my
Dear, would be
Without these special
pondering.

How sterile a life-
unsavory
Without some certain
memories
To mingle
And to dance
Within these massive
trees.

Love doeth transcend
time and toil,
Lingers long...
Beyond the mundane
emptiness of this mortal
coil.

Fall is in the Air
August 28 2010

Fall is in the air today.
Leaves changing. All
can see.
Geese are training
in a "vee.."

Salmon swimming home
to spawn
Pine odor brisk among
the trees
Brown ferns rough
against my knees.
Summer's warm will
soon be gone.

Grasses die before 'ere
long
Robins flock for long
flight south,
Peck worms to fill an
anxious mouth
I miss their limpid song.

Carefree swims and
camping gone

School supplies are in
the stores
Rigid schedules, home
bound chores
Student life finds
one alone

Cord-wood stacks must
be accrued
Six month's fuel with
sharpened tool
Demand spare moments
that's
the rule
For fireplace so much
imbued.

Autumn's onset up-north
call for
Canning goods the
farmers haul
Beans carrots and corn
so tall
Winter's tasty
veggies all

Vacant boat slips
indicate
Vessels prep their winter
wait
While mooring docks
prepare for ice
Close friend who
snuggles much too tight

Change of season 'tis
good reason
Up-north citizens
engage

A dance to duties of the
day
Tuned to Nature's
turning page

This one chapter comes
to end.
Summer yields around
the bend
To chilly chimes- the
Mother's "gift"
Tour first ice and ten foot
drift.

False Information From Fall
October 20, 2010

One blustery day I heard
that fall
Would like to mummify
us all-
Long stockings up a
drafty shin
Attaching mosses to our
skin.

Fall interrupts a
summer's peace
To misdirect large flocks
of geese
By charting flights to
southern burgh.
Tells diesel fuel it's time
to curd.

Gives clouds of rain
some chilling tale

That turns their droplets
into hail.
Fall's latest nasty caper,
Informs Jack Frost he's
out of paper.

Shocks flocks of ducks
with,"Time
to go!"
Turns ear and nose
to indigo.
Give lies to noble oaken
trees
enough to make them
shed their leaves.

Confuses cats about
their hair
Asides all squirrels to go
hide nuts.

Spreads lies to deer to
start their ruts.
I feel that fall just
isn't fair!

Autumn too is out there
lying,
Whispers to graceful
maple trees
Convincing them to drop
their leaves

Just so he can hear
them crying.

Fall and autumn
dastardly
Spread such dirt to have
their way
Jealous of our joyful
summer
Bent on making us look
dumber.

Forest Floor
October 18, 2010

Forest floor lies silent
now.
Golden rays filter down
through their canopy
Casting patchwork
shadows
Along my carpet of pine
smelling bows.

Breathless down I lie
Near Dad's old deer
blind,
Hands under head,
Toward a robin-egg sky.

Shack's unattended,
save a grandson or two
Window pane cracks let
autumn mice through.
Potbellied stove lost it's
rusty stove pipe
While tears come and

flow with eloquent wipe.

Lone chickadee peeps
As he flits near my head
Recalling at large
What Dad always said:

"Deer are a curious sort
But with luck,
Follow the does
For you'll soon see the
buck.

Eat Limburger cheese
With onion to please.
Let's a buck know
That he has a new doe.

Deer are a curious sort
They'll sneak on up
With the wind and give
snort.

While hunting with skill.

So, snap back the
safety.
Take careful aim.
Hit his front shoulder.
You got venison game!"

Both needed to exit
That feminine house
For wing-shot bagging
Of pheasant or grouse.

Hemingway also had
that to feel
When doctor Dad
Taught gun safety

Mourning dove, white tail
Black bear or squirrels
Father/son mastery
Was not for his girls.

Harbor Springs...Late Fall
October 20, 2008

Morning mist doeth
hover now
Casting Springs(Harbor
Springs) in eerie glow.
Weak morning sun
burns off some spell
That mid-night spun
upon this strand so tall.

Thick frosty nights doeth
gild our fickle land
Where elfin Jack has
tried his fancy hand
To decorate and best
God's golden leaves
That still refuse to fall.

Children anxious (inward
scream)
Do dance, indeed to
leap this Halloween,
To frighten sister's little
thugs
Then calming them with
gentle hugs...
Exciting is the scene.

Come carve with me a

jack-o-lant'
Then save for Lent his
slippery seeds
While conjuring what vile
new tricks
Will best our last, past
dastard' deeds.

Now hark!
Do drum and time now
toll?
Neath, Harbor Springs'
cold Gothic pall,
Mid spook, with chime
and chilly clime,
Brings Chippewa with
classic shawl,

Who feed the fallen's
favorite dish
To sing, to break fry-
bread and fish
Observing custom's call.
What tribal natives call,
"dagwaagi",
White -folk call... late
fall.

<u>Last Day of Indian Summer</u>
November 16, 2010

Morning sun glimmers on stout mufti-colored leaves that
still cling to dormant trees and bushes. Strong shafts of
morning sunlight penetrate mist-filled gullies intent upon
dissolving what remains of fragile evening gossamer.

A fine blanket of shimmering stillness hangs heavily
along the edge of Old Tannery Creek as each gurgle
and murmur of the fast-moving brook sadly announce
the end of our brief but glorious Indian Summer.
Small swarms of tiny midge try to get in one more
delicate dance floating upon the whispers of warm,
magical, Autumn air. They mirror the puff-tops of seed-
laden weed stalks which hang illumined by back light
from the morning dawn.

Reminds me of Aunt Helen in her handmade lace shawl
as she slowly strolls, hunched over, among her dying
flowerbeds drinking her morning Postum while talking to
Uncle Alfred who died in her bed ten years ago.
In the distance muffled sounds of rifle shots remind us
that deer hunters also share our mystical mornings as
they try to remove the prince of these pristine
surroundings.

Ernest Hemingway began his famous writing career
among these same inspiring sanctuaries one hundred
years ago. Entering the solitude and solemnity of the
then virgin timbers made him think he was in God's
towering cathedral. That Nick Adams character brings
out this fact many times during adventures in colorful
northern Michigan. He had twenty inspiring years to
enjoy our enchanted forests.

Oh, Righteous Wind
October 31, 2010

Oh, righteous wind
Come blow within
Clear clutter from our
hearts.

Blow ever billowy,
baneful blasts
Like leaves across the
grass.

Blow doubt away
Leave joy and peace
Transform my world
today.

Oh, righteous wind
Come blow within
To calm a restless mind.

If love would hide
Free flocks of dove
To spread the message
wide.

Ignite a flame
Atop my brain
To trigger agape love

Extinguish controversial
blame
My heavenly goal the
gain.

Oh, righteous wind
Come blow within.
Extinguish sin I pray,
Until I win against
the Foe
To have a perfect day.

Oh, bless my daily food
always.
Condition me to give.
Be more like Christ
My new-found friend
Who makes me
truly live.

<u>Release of the Milkweed Pod</u>
October 19, 2010

I walked a windy autumn
path
That found me cutting
'crossed a field
Which like a child this
morning hath
Lead to stalks revealed.

Their sun-dried casing
caught mine eye,
For sixty years ago did I
Thrill to tear their pear-
shaped crusty bod
Releasing seeds within
the milkweed pod.

With childish wonder
assumed dim
It struck to thrill me once
again
As scores of silken seed
trapped in
Caught this brisk
October wind.

Burst forth from confined

cells did they
Like miners trapped all
summer lay
Etching futures bright
some say
Then spread as puffs of
cosmic white sachet.

Their silky heirs sought
broader fairs
Propelled by stiff
autumnal airs
To live again abundantly
like our sweet Lord
intended.

And so go I
As God did see
Imprisoned by my sin.
Then comes God's Son
who took my place
Like autumn's righteous
wind
To bless the cloistered
world I face
And free us from within!

Scantily Clad Elms
September 29. 2010

Scantily clad elms now
quake-
Their dying amber duds
do shake
In homage to the colder
nights.
In duty bow toward
winter's somber wake.

Rusty ovals flutter by
Her great pulsations fill a
sky
Rude strip of gown
Cleft autumn's pallet
puckish brown.
Fall's curious cold fronts
Who reach in
Seem lost
Yet know must chill her
skin
Grown tender now from
summer's fondling
palms.

Coy elms be-muse,
"How can this be?"
Bare breasts abused
Sway pendulous.
Is weather ever un-
excused?

Fall rears his fickle
flanks
He bears her shoulder
cold which ranks
Near jilted maiden
feeling strong,
Ex-lover's parting, swan-
like song.

Long necked geese hear
summer's wail
Will wag a sympathetic
tail
While lining dutifully
In artful Vee for
southward plow.

A heart doeth burst!
What could be worse?
(As summer gives long
acquiescent heaves),
Than barren elms now
taken shy
('Gainst autumn's
scandalous, grey eye)
Stripped naked of her
lovely leaves.

Significance of Having a History
November 2, 2010

A life without a sense of
the past
Is a life which feels it will
not belong-
Rootless, clueless if at
best,
An awkward dance
without a song.

Overlooking Harbor
Springs
My heart invariably
starts to sing
When my history comes
to mind...
Of attitudes of a
wholesome kind.

Dusty, moldy, photo
books
Show round-faced girls
in full-length dresses,
Braided, full-length,

natural tresses,
High-heeled shoes with
button hooks,
Of chaperones with
studied looks.

Chivalry had manners
there,
Romance had men who
really care,
Built their goods of a
lasting kind,
Honored a life with me in
mind.

Gave birth to more than
two or three
For strengthening our
family tree.
Built stout boats from
bark of birch
Their life course beg,an
in church.

In Search of The Kingdom
(November 10, 2010)

Where can I find it?
I ask myself and God.
My dear Lord,
May I somehow
Get a glimpse of your
Kingdom?

Are you in this flock
Of long necked geese
Who bob in the bay?
This triple-trunk birch
Which begins to sway?

Would you be in

This wrinkled old LT Bay
Which gives in
To each troubling wind?
Would you ever consider
This grey pile of limestone
Which we have for a
beach?

Or me in my white suit
Eating a peach?

Or the crippled girl
Longingly paging through
Glam-our?

Or the truck traffic
Causing such incessant
clamber?

Maybe in the crashing
waterfall
Which I hear from behind,

Or maybe it was my

waitress
Just being kind?

Mine eyes will behold you
Some day I am sure.
That day will be crystal,
Flawless and pure.

Oh!... There!
I just saw you!
In the Great Wheel
-The Sun-
Setting behind condos
On His cross-continent
run.

It was love at first light
Free energy, thee!
It was there all along.

For you and for me...

God's Solar Love Song!

Walking Sails Along the Edge
October 3, 2010

Summer's last sailboat,
today
Sliced silently a jagged
swath
Disturbing a solitude
blue bay.

Odious sails catch
pompous puffs of
autumn air-

Last free forces fair-
Last clutching snare
Of ready main 'mid
willing, jealous jib.

Taught rides this sturdy
canvas lair.
Full leans sleek craft
'mid vacant stare.
Last thrill 'till spring-

Then six month stale- air
crib.

More lean just makes
him feel alive.
Continues through each
awesome jibe
As fabrics tighten when
she comes about.

Cleft wider vees
In wake now aft.
As waves of laugh
Wet-slap, her jutting,
eager bow

While frightened foam
and fervent eddy
Try to match each furrow
Of his sweaty brow.

But winds subside,
As does his pride
Seen glorious now
Considering this time.

So late:
To venture out so far!
To tempt a Neptune by
this tar!
So late to pit a duel with
Mother N.

Next year he'll try his fit
again
Will edge-walk sailing
never end?
Or will Poseidon odds
catch up with him?

Waltz of the Sea Birds
October 20, 2004

Brisk breezes lift my
cap,
Inflate my unsnapped
wrap
And spur me on to skip
my nap;
As I stroll 'long Little
Traverse Bay.

Observe the fine array of
festooned fowl
Congregating in a bowl
For midday bath with
gossip-
Friendly goose-chatter
filled with meaning
Midst their nervous,
mindless preening.

Herring gulls stand-by
and wait
Watching ganders
congregate
Know full well this beach
Will soon be theirs
alone...but late.

Water levels sink below
Exposing seaweed rich
and show
How God takes care
Of every hair and
feather,
More than arbitrary flow
of weather.

Rotting leaves play their
part
After bold exhibit Art
Decompose and
become food for thought
What our great God hath
wrought.

Off-shore billows lend a
hand
Exposing ancient
heirloom sand...
Tasty lunch for coot or
crane,
Microbes sweet as sugar
cane.

Market report does not
retort
Nor indicate our grand
resort-
Our love affair
With Nature's music in
the air.

Mallard 'ganzer, tern and
stork,
Heron, mud hen, snipe
and wren
All on God depend,
Find their food 'round
every bend.

Mother Nature's

delicatessen
Serves us right to learn
this lesson-
Though they look as if
they're bored,
Birds have faith and do
not hoard.

Israel, Esther, Jude and
Hannah,
Every morning plucked
their Manna,
Giving thanks for what
they had,

Knew full well that had
they stashed it,
Next day it would all go
bad.

Lots to learn
At every turn!
Stop and burn this
memory
Deep within each
mammary…
God's alive and He's well.
Cares for all; as one can
tell.

When Rocks Will Talk
October 26, 2004

As I pondered late, I queried-
Nature's wonders some have theoried.
Are all accident.
End of story,
There.
But, yet...

Can we rob God of His glory?
As we survey all our region
Untold beauty comes by legion
Counting resource
That we get.

If we did not laud and honor,
Surely, He (God) would start to wonder,
"Where are all the thank yous
From my progeny?"

If we did not shout His praise
Serious doubts our silence raise,
That every rock would surely shout!
Gems would dance and jump about!

Quartz and sapphire would take wing.
Amethyst would surely sing,
"Praises be to God, oh earth,
From the arctic down to Perth!"

Every turquoise, fossil'd tril'bite,
Agate, ruby, topaz, calcite,
Every rock from every nation,
All would praise Thee in ovation.

Humble grasses that thou made
Stand erect, yes, every blade
Pointing skyward; as to say
"Father, hear my praise today!"

Boulders, gravel, would unravel
Litany beyond compare,
Pyrite organs pipe the aire,
"God hath blessed beyond compare."

If this geologic nation
Raised their voices in
oblation,
What does our church
then have to say?
Is this Pentecostal Day?

If we're united in one
spirit.
Filled with love and need
to share it,
Rock the rafters, sister,

brother!
Chime in, Father, blend
with, Mother!

Join with rocks and
natural wonder
Deep within this "crusty
blunder."
Let this be our 'piphany-
One triumphant
symphony!

Editorial comment:

(It should be pointed out that science is indeed using rocks and gems in numerous ways for communication purposes. Quartz crystals make radio possible, rubies are the main stay in laser technology, and humble sand (silicone) is the source for micro technology which drives today's computer industry and crosses our oceans riding on millions of miles of fiber optic cables).

Truly Jesus' prediction -that if we did not shout His praises, the very stones would indeed cry out-(Luke 19-40) has come true. This is spiritual irony of the highest order. Praise the Lord!

Epilogue

Throughout his adult life, Hemingway had shorted himself in the area of religion. Much to his chagrin it eventually led to his demise. Religion would have kept him from insanity.

We saw a serious deterioration of his sparkling personality and sharp plot choices out of step with the changing times. In fact he got a bit crazy in the latter quadrant of his exciting life. Had he used his genius to pursue the meaning of life, God would have abundantly revealed Himself. Unfortunately he did not and we lost a great talent.

His writing had lost its luster and vitality, sinking deeply into the dark world of his personal demons. His latter work reveals a non characteristic delving into a shadowy closet of the kinky, obsessed with the bizarre world of trans-gender bedroom role-playing in order to stimulate a rejuvenation of his dwindling libido.

A personal walk with the Lord would have protected his mind from being invaded by the demonic. A daily delving into the Word would have built a hedge of psychic security around his mind that would have produced an inspiring wisdom and perception, transforming his later writing style.

With just a cursory understanding of vital spiritual knowledge Holy ritual; Holy Baptism, Holy Eucharist, Marriage, and prayer, Ernest's genius could not be maintained and was wasted.

Ernie's constant search for community would have been found at church, where he needed to worship God and give God the glory for his writing talent. Joining a loving congregation anchored in the Word would have cured his anxieties and awarded him some peace through humility and devotion to God.

Eventually his reliance on writing as Journal Therapy, de-stressers of ritualistic fishing and hunting, ingesting copious amounts of mind-numbing alcohol all began to wear thin. His home grown form of "alternative religion" born out of the Roaring Twenties of which he was self proclaimed High Priest, came crashing down on him, metaphor for the many plane and car crashes he suffered.(see "Sun Also Rises"...fishing trip)

Having no device to use against his build-up of guilt, Hemingway foundered. He became a loose cannon endangering the vulnerable deck hands of his ship-of-state.

Toward the end even America's best clinics had no pill, no workable technique, no magic potion to calm his troubled mind. Convulsive electro-shock destroyed his memory making writing impossible . Desperate to silence that chattering demon-controlled mind that constantly condemned him, reminding him unendingly of the shambles he had made of his family life and literary profession, the satanic voices called for the permanent shutting up that only suicide could provide and he tragically obeyed.

The key to the elaborate arsenal locked in his gun case was placed in plain sight (a detail Miss Mary could never explain truthfully knowing he had tried unsuccessfully many times before) so the "ultimate prey" that alluded him all his life was actually he...himself!

But this sad tale could have been avoided and in my small way, through my poetry ,written in the spirit of the youthful Hemingway, I attempt to expand and redirect his vision praying that you, dear reader, will see the error of this fun filled hedonistic life style

By expanding on themes written during his youthful Petoskey-innocence I show the reader how it could have been.

Herein, we get a glimpse of a life revisited in a body of work done "properly", the way Ernest would have wanted it, had he been loyal to the Lord of his youth.

Captives
by Ernest Hemingway

Some came in chains
Unrepentant but tired.
Too tired but to stumble.
Thinking and hating were finished
Thinking and fighting were finished
Retreating and hoping were finished.
ᐧong campaign, Making death easy.[17]

BASEBOARD

KYTRIL®
granisetron HCl
Tablets and Injection

Author Biography

David Henry Wyant, M.Ed. was born in Rogers City Michigan, just 60 miles directly east of Petoskey, along Lake Huron. He graduated with honors from RCHS in 1959 during a time when most young Americans strongly felt the need to do what they could to beat Russia into outer space. At seventeen, he drew rocket plans for NASA.

A graduate of Concordia University, Chicago(Bible College,BA) and Wayne State Univ. Detroit, MI,(MA), Mr. Wyant taught elementary school for 30 years specializing in Art. He worked on a team which wrote the state Art curriculum for Florida.

He currently enjoys visits with his daughter, Lisa Luebke (wife of Randall), five grandchildren and one great grandchild who all live nearby in Boyne City, Michigan. Inspired by the seasonal drama of Petsokey's ever changing natural beauty, Art teacher, Wyant, shows us how to paint with words. Experiencing this body of work strikes a colorful chord on many levels including some of our deepest spiritual aspects. Never dry nor pedantic, many vibrant, deeply personal passages are delivered with a special charm and whimsey. David's rhythms are as fluid as the Bear River which flows next to his apartment. He translates the flow of our natural world into one's deeply personal history. Timely brassy phrasings reveal his intimate understanding of symphonic music as an outstanding trumpet player in high school and college. Experiencing Petoskey will never be the same after you read, "The Town That Haunted Hemingway". David's first books were "My Petoskey 'Stones'" and "A Compilation of Poems".

Mr. Wyant is available for readings of his books, writer's workshops and readings of his unique regional poetry.

To contact Author David Wyant and for more information on his other books, visit him at his website:

www.wizardofwalloon.com

Further Reading

Stolen in Paris:The Lost Chronicles of Young Ernest Hemingway, by David H. Wyant.

"The Lost Chronicles hits home with the teenage genius search for truth in all of us."

The Hemingways had everything 1900's life had to offer, but it wasn't enough for their genius teenaged son, Ernest.

Fueled by his overactive imagination, his devil-may-care attitude, together with too much late night consumption of classic adventure stories, Ernie and his friends and siblings embark upon a tumultuous, highly-stoked summer, deep into virgin forests of wild, untamed Petoskey, Michigan.

Ernest Hemingway's first wife, Hadley, lost a suitcase full of prized manuscripts on a trip home from Paris in 1921. These missing stories were never to be seen again. Who knows what literary classics that suitcase may have contained?

In the imagination of this author have been found those missing memoirs—a series of fourteen exciting adventures, with more to come, found by way of "biographic fantasy noir." "The Lost Chronicles of Young Ernest Hemingway" unveil his earliest, most fascinating adventure stories, and monologues read like eaves-dropping while he unloads in his priest's confessional booth. The author imagines what the childhood and teenage life of Ernest Hemingway in Petoskey must have been like.

This stylish series of young adult novels reveals literary merit, fine design, and strong kid-relevance. Filled with unbridled Victorian romance, adventure, betrayal, parent-sibling drama, and tribal temptations tastefully presented like a cathartic, primal glimpse into one, very troubled, sub-conscious.

"History comes alive in these historical adventure stories!"

The Lost Chronicles of Young Ernest Hemingway is indeed the perfect platform on which to expose those early, deeply gnarled roots of America's most analyzed, literary bad boy.

Find them all on ebook today! Available at: Amazon.com, BN.com, and Smashwords.com

Endnotes

1. Idema, H. 1990. "Freud, Religion, and the Roaring Twenties: A Psychoanalytic Theory of Secularization in Three Novelists : Anderson, Hemingway, and Fitzgerald", Rowman & Littlefield. Pages 135-176.
2. Adams, J. 2011. Petoskey, Michigan.
3. Mellow, J. 1992. "Hemingway: A Life Without Consequences". New York: Houghton Mifflin.
4. Miller, J. 2009. "He Re-wrote History". MyNorth. <http://www.mynorth.com/My-North/June-2009/He-Rewrote-History>
5. Indiana University -Purdue University Fort Wayne. "Grant and Lee: A Study in Contrasts. Bruce Catton". <http://users.ipfw.edu/ruflethe/grantandlee.html>
6. Baker, C. 1981. "Ernest Hemingway Selected Letters 1917-1961." Scribner's Publishing. Pages 136-137.
7. Gerogiannis, N. 1983. "Complete Poems of Ernest Hemingway." Page 5.
8. Ibid. Page 13.
9. Harry S. Truman Library and Museum, Kansas City Star Building. <http://www.trumanlibrary.org/places/kc1.htm>
10. Baker, C. 1981. "Ernest Hemingway Selected Letters 1917-1961." Scribner's Publishing. Page 14.
11. Baker, C. 1981. "Ernest Hemingway Selected Letters 1917-1961." Charles Scribner's and Son's Publishing. Page 20.
12. Gerogiannis, N. 1983. "Complete Poems of Ernest Hemingway."
13. Montgomery, C. C. 1966. "Hemingway in Michigan." Fleet

Publishing Corporation. Page 168.

14. Ibid.

15. Ibid

16. Hemingway, E. 1954. "Torrents of Spring." Arrow Books.

17. Gerogiannis, N. 1983. "Complete Poems of Ernest Hemingway."

18. Ibid. Page 85.

19. Ibid. Page 86

20. Montgomery, C. C. 1966. "Hemingway in Michigan." Fleet Publishing Corporation. Page 166.

21. Hemingway, E. 1954. "Torrents of Spring." Arrow Books.

22. Gerogiannis, N. 1983. "Complete Poems of Ernest Hemingway." Page 51.

23. Ibid. Page 29.

24. Ibid. Page 30.

25. Ibid. Page 31.

26. Ibid. Page 33.

27. Ibid. Page 36.

28. Ibid. Page 37.

29. Ibid. Page 40.

30. Ibid. Page 41.

31. Ibid. Page 42.

32. Ibid. Page 43.

33. Ibid. Page 45.

34. Ibid. Page 46.

35. Ibid. Page 47

36. Ibid. Page 49.

37. Ibid. Page 50.

38. Ibid. Page 53.

39. Ibid. Page 57.

40. Ibid. Page 62.

41. Ibid. Page 65.

42. Ibid. Page 83.

43. Ibid. Page 125.